Boxing the Compass

OCCASIONAL PAPERS IN FOLKLORE
No. 6

GIBB SCHREFFLER

Boxing the Compass

A Century and a Half of Discourse About Sailors' Chanties

CAMSCO Music
1308 Brittany Pointe
Lansdale, PA 19446
800-548-FOLK

Loomis House Press
www.loomishousepress.com

ISBN 978-1-935243-81-6

CONTENTS

Introduction: Finding True North   1

   I   Observations of Contemporaries (1850s–1880s)   6

  II   Early Collections (1880s–90s)   24

 III   Remembering Across the 19th–20th-century Divide   30

 IV   The Emergence of Folklore Studies (1900s–1910s)   45

  V   Resources for Revival (1910s–1940s)   57

 VI   Developments in Folklore Studies (1920s–1960s)   69

 VII   The Final Seal: Stan Hugill   83

VIII   Post-Hugill Studies (1960s–2010s)   90

Concluding Note   97

References   101

INTRODUCTION: FINDING TRUE NORTH

How do we know what we know about chanties? Most people, if they have any concept of a chanty, will know it as a type of sailor-song, perhaps knowing it more specifically to be a work-song. They will probably envision some sort of person whom they imagine to be the typical singer of chanties, and hold some notion, however vague, of the age of these songs and their typical musical characteristics. Depending in large part on one's age and the geography of one's upbringing, most will have formed their picture of what chanties are from such sources as fiction films, amusement parks, maritime museums, and popular music scenes.

In my case—so far as my imagination assists me in remembering—my upbringing in the 1970s–80s in Hartford County, Connecticut, being close enough to the Mystic Seaport Museum and in a state that retained a certain maritime identity, would have been enough to expose me to the idea of "chanties" before ever realizing it was something that people born elsewhere would have never heard of until conversing with me on the subject. When first did my exposure to chanties take place? I would have heard chanties in trips to the Seaport both inside and outside of school. Perhaps we sang them in school, as chanties have long been a popular choice of repertoire for educators. I certainly attended "folk music" concerts in which locals engaged with "sea music," such as Don Sineti of my hometown of Bloomfield, peppered their sets with chanty items. And I can only assume that all manner of media—novels, Saturday morning cartoons, crossword puzzles—reinforced or added to my personal epistemological development with respect to "chanty." Yet I cannot remember one moment when the concept of a "chanty" was introduced to me, or for that matter when I was taught to *pronounce* it; I always already knew it, as if it had been a regular part of my enculturation as a New Englander in the late twentieth century. My parents' generation were well familiarized with at least one item of chanty repertoire, "Blow the Man Down"; I believe they inherited this knowledge, with the help of old films, from their own parent's generation, the so-called Greatest Generation, for whom those old films were produced, and all of whom I imagine to have been pretty gung-ho for seafaring icons of a naval variety. Because my own family did not participate in the Anglophone Folk Revival (wherein chanties made up a bonafide subcategory of songs), but they did serve in the military (my grandfather was in the U.S.

Merchant Marine) it was through absorption from pop culture and military service that my ancestors likely constructed their concept of chanties.

Indeed, born for the most part the children of immigrants to America in the years during or just after World War I, my grandparents possessed a knowledge of chanties that would have already developed considerably since the genre's heyday in merchant sailing vessels. Consider the fact that people have been studying and performing sailors' chanties outside of their original, shipboard context for at least as long as the songs were ever used to accompany labor tasks in that context itself. Therefore, the concepts of chanties that we have tended to inherit derive mostly from discourse that has taken place outside the "native" site of performance and that has been produced by people with no experience of that space. In the vast majority of cases, our sources of information to attach to the word "chanty"—whether it be a *Pirates of the Caribbean* amusement encountered on a family vacation to Disneyland or Hugill's *Shanties from the Seven Seas*, purchased on Amazon after playing the video game *Assassin's Creed IV: Black Flag*—are based in other sources that are in turn based in other sources, and so on. Second hand, third hand, fourth hand. It may not be turtles *all* the way down, but the turtles do go on for a bit before one reaches the level of experiential knowledge—the knowing of chanties first and foremost as tools one learned to use at the same time as one learned to work a ship. And yet this is not to say that sailing a windjammer is what it takes to "properly" know chanties, or that those who sail today are closer to "true" knowledge of the genre. Modern sailing crews, who rarely employ chanties and even more rarely do so with both an informed approach to their practice and under the same conditions as 19th-century tars, generally differ little from landlubbers in their ways of knowing the genre. From a theoretical standpoint it is not possible to know chanties just as the early generations knew them, as understandings have inevitably developed under the influence of so many intervening events. Our understandings come from, are shaped by, a discourse, which, like the current and wind bear upon a ship's course, is constantly altered by social currents and the winds of ideology.

Readers at this point should not fear the academic-sounding word *discourse*. I use it only to mean the verbal communication of, and exchange of ideas about, a particular topic (in this case, chanties). I use the word discourse because, whereas much of this survey does deal with communication in print, the larger picture of knowledge production and transmission includes oral communication in conversations, presentations, and performances, and thus a more inclusive term is needed. "Discourse" also suggests a back-and-forth, an exchange between participants who produce discourse and whom may simply be called discussants. My aim is not a complex theoretical analysis of this discourse—ambitious readers are welcome to pursue that themselves—but rather, primarily, to *map* it.

Discussants of chanty history, today, are not only separated from historical knowing of their subject by time—at least a century—but also by what one might call the layers of prior discourse. These layers entail an accumulation, like geological strata. (Mis)conception and (mis)perception, biases of nationality, race, class, and education, forgetting and denial of forgetting, rationalization and idealization, representation and presentation, practical issues of function and communication, and so many other reasons to objectify and discuss chanties have created these layers. This book may yet be another.

In undertaking this effort I assume that there are people interested in improving our understanding the chanty genre as an historical subject, and that research to that end will continue. With that in mind, the purpose of the mapping exercise of this work is to identify the layers and, hopefully, to aid scholars to see both what is beneath them and how they affect contemporaneous evidence. Only then does the historical evidence have a chance of shining through and we can reconstruct the best picture of chanties in their heyday. Perhaps it is less like cleaning a window than restoring an old painting. One cannot simply wipe the slate. For the knowledge we do want to find is layered as well. To do the former, one might accept only primary sources that are more or less contemporaneous with the practices they describe. In fact, these are among the valuable sources for new historical work on the subject. However, most writers will also want to carefully use sources somewhat more removed—and thus mixed in with subsequent layers of discourse—because they offer so much more information, even if they sacrifice immediacy.

To elaborate further on the need for this work: I contend that the people who have been discussing chanties in the last fifty years or so have mostly been working (extending the geological dig metaphor) at the "surface." The general assumption, perhaps—and not an unreasonable one—is that with each successive writer on chanty-singing since the initial demise of the practice in the merchant ships, knowledge has increased. Information certainly has, but understanding remains to drift on its own course while the view behind is obscured by effects of time and bias. In my observation, discussants tend to begin with what they have heard said around them, moving then to the works of the early to mid-twentieth century—from which much of the hearsay had come in the first place. The popular written works appear either to confirm the hearsay or challenge it in a self-deceptive way. A certain consistency between popular works leads them to being interpreted as corroborating facts; surprisingly few readers seem to interpret this evidence of consistency as an indication of cross-influence, uncritical scholarship, or even plagiarism. In another scenario, when one of these problematic work says something contrary to current hearsay, it may be invested with a renewed sense of authenticity. This inconsistency becomes yet another truism: that due to oral transmission there were many "versions" of chanties—"Different ships, different long splices," is the adage. Yet the authors of many of these books, which are on the shelves of chanty enthusiasts and consulted with fair reverence, did not scratch very deeply beneath the surface of the seemingly authentic sources they, caught in their own discourse, had at hand. A bottleneck forms around the turn of the twentieth century, effectively sealing off insight available in 19th-century sources. I say the nineteenth century was "sealed off" not only due to the once more limited accessibility to its sources, but also because the 20th-century sources, with their widespread neglect of earlier writing and their more cogent and attractive manner of presentation, gave off the appearance that prior knowledge was naïve and obsolete.

The alternative way to gain an understanding of chanty history, today, is not to begin digging through the top layers downwards, but rather to approach the subject from "below"—as one tunes a fiddle string by first going below the desired pitch and then "tuning up." The method of this book then is to tune up the discourse about chanties by beginning with the early sources, even if they may seem to be less informative or comprehensive. Building from there, I map the discourse chronologically to understand subsequent discussions in terms of how they may have been determined by those prior. Only then can we judge whether a writer is likely stating an original idea or an independent observation of practice, or whether he or she has adopted questionable information and ideas introduced in prior discourse. This path is far from straight; each writing, naturally, does not build directly on others. Some writings are nearly all derivative while others are mostly original. Yet even the ones with the most original information and statements were conceived within some established discursive frame.

This survey is not exhaustive. The literature and scholarly activity addressed herein is that which in some way addresses chanties directly and substantially. Many more works, indeed, *mention* chanties in passing; these, in fact, constitute much of that body of primary and contemporary evidence that must be employed in future histories of the genre. Further, the survey cannot cover every such secondary source. In particular, those sources that appear to be mainly derivative or unoriginal, or else which have little impact on discourse, have been omitted. Finally, because the main objective is to sort through this discourse with an eye to viewing information on the historical chanty practice, discursive products that mainly reveal "revival" or latter-day practices (an interesting, but different topic) have been neglected.

Despite these limitations, this work intends to be useful to anyone seeking to enter a scholarly conversation about sailors' chanties. The discourse it covers spans a century and a half and includes *most* of the works and perspectives on chanties that one is likely to encounter. The reader will become familiar with the major names of authors and sources—boxing the compass, as it were. By situating the past works within the context of developing layers of discourse, the present work is a guide to where to go for certain types of information while avoiding the pitfalls inherent to such a complex history of knowledge production.

With these caveats, let us proceed in the spirit of constructive critique. The goal is not to invalidate ways of knowing chanties, but to hone our ability to create new insight through a rigorous examination of perspectives.

I — OBSERVATIONS OF CONTEMPORARIES (1850s–1880s)

We begin with the seminal discourse to focus on the topic of chanties. At this time, the 1850s to 1880s, chanties had yet to become framed as belonging to any canon of national or "folk" music. These authors were writing neither as promoters nor as researchers, but rather as observers of then-current chanty-singing. Their impressions would have been informed by chanties' living style and manner of performance during the genre's heyday. In this respect, we can suppose they reflect some of the original or early cultural connotations that chanties held.

Mention of sailor work-songs similar to or corresponding to chanties began to occur in works of the 1830s, including Dana's well-known travelogue, *Two Years Before the Mast* (1840), and the anonymous account of a "Steerage passenger" on an East Indiaman voyage, *The Quid* (1832). These works stand out, on the one hand, due to the silence about such songs in such contexts in the prior decades' writing. On the other hand, the repertoire they present appears to have been either forgotten within a few decades (and thus unknown to us at present) or else survived only in patches. Moreover, during the 1830s and 1840s, work-songs were mentioned only incidentally within such narratives as these. Being primary sources and not focused substantially on the discussing the topic, these are beyond the scope of this survey.

> *It is not recreation; it is an essential part of the work.*
> —*The Atlantic Monthly*, July 1858

The first works to address the maritime work-songs as a discrete topic came in 1858, at a time which the phenomenon still had not, evidently, received a universally known name.[1] The first of these discussions came in a July 1858 issue of the Boston-based periodical *The Atlantic Monthly*, where an anonymous author wrote on "Songs of the Sea." He (I presume the gender) first explains how, in contrast to military ships, songs were needed on merchant ships.

> Merchantmen are invariably manned with the least possible number, and often go to sea shorthanded, even according to the parsimonious calculations of their owners. The only way the heavier work can be

done at all is by each man doing his utmost at the same moment. This is regulated by the song. And here is the true singing of the deep sea. It is not recreation; it is an essential part of the work. It mastheads the topsail-yards, on making tail; it starts the anchor from the domestic or foreign mud; it "rides down the main tack with a will"; it breaks out and takes on board cargo; it keeps the pumps…going. A good voice and a new and stirring chorus are worth an extra man. And there is plenty of need of both.[2]

Thus the *Atlantic Monthly* writer establishes the sailor's work-song as a category of its own—a tool of its own. He then presents an anecdote, ostensibly, from his own experience, of how the song "Haul on the Bowline" was used to board tacks and sheets, with the unanimous pull on the final word of the chorus, "haul!"

The English second-mate was stamping with vexation, and, with all his Hs misplaced… "Give us the song, men!" sang out the mate, at last,— "pull with a will!—together, men!—haltogether now!"—And then a cracked, melancholy voice struck up this chant:

"Oh, the bowline, bully bully bowline,
Oh, the bowline, bowline, HAUL!"

At the last word every man threw his whole strength into the pull,— all singing it in chorus, with a quick, explosive sound…I dare say this will seem very much spun out to a seafarer, but landsmen like to hear of the sea and its ways; and as more landsmen than seamen, probably, read the "Atlantic Monthly," I have told them of one genuine sea-song, and its time and place.[3]

This presumably American writer goes on to mention the tasks of pumping and halyards, and to quote phrases or verses from four other songs known as "chanties" to us today. An organized exposition it is not, but it was first to present the topic as one of interest to laypeople.

*...I cannot help noticing the similarity existing
between the working chorus of the sailors
and the dirge-like negro melody...*
—I. Allen, December 1858

The other article of 1858 came out in December, in Oberlin College's monthly student publication. The contributor, Isaac Allen, wrote about "Songs of the Sailor." Allen appears to be writing from first hand experience, although perhaps from only one voyage. Nonetheless, his writing is reflective, painting his impressions of the sights and sounds of sailor labor. He quotes three familiar chanties, and a fourth which, though not corresponding exactly to a distinct canonical item, is unmistakably cut from the cloth of the chanty genre:

> We've a bully ship and a bully crew,
>   Heigho, heave and go;
> We've a bully mate and a captain too;
>   Heigho, heave and go.[4]

What is most remarkable about Allen's article is the author's reflection that the sailor work-songs sounded like African-American songs. He first says,

> But strange as it may seem, however varied the appearance and nationality of the ship and its crew, be they from Archangel's icebound coast, or India's coral strand, Saxon or Celt, Frenchman or Turk, Russian or African, we invariably find that the strain of the sailor's work-song has the same plaintive minor key, strongly reminding one of their similarity in this respect to the sad-toned melodies of the negro race.[5]

The Oberlin author goes on to relate an anecdote of a Black shipmate singing his "country song," supposedly mistaken by the other crew for weeping, in order to make the broader point that the songs of African-descended people everywhere shared a similar quality.

> Along the African coast you will hear that dirge-like strain in all their songs, as at work or paddling their canoes to and from shore, they keep time to the music. On the southern plantations you will hear it also, and in the negro melodies every where, plaintive and melodious, sad and earnest. It seems like the dirge of national degradation, the wail of a race, stricken and crushed, familiar with tyranny, submission and unrequited labor.

And here I cannot help noticing the similarity existing between the working chorus of the sailors and the dirge-like negro melody...[6]

What follows is Allen's sort of phenomenological proof of the relation between sailor work-songs and "African" songs. He relates that his ship was once at anchor somewhere, where the main population of the land was of African descent. The ship was approached by the canoes of "natives," while at the same time the crew heard "a well known strain of music." At first they thought that another ship was weighing anchor, that is, that another crew was singing a chanty. Then they realized that it was the canoe rowers keeping time with their paddles to

Heigh Jim along, Jim along Josey, Heigh Jim along, Jim along Jo![7]

Evidently Allen did not recognize this as a relative of the published minstrel song "Jim Along Josey" (1840).[8] Yet nor can we be sure that the minstrel song was not originally fashioned after a traditional one. I suggest there was more to this performance than the lyrics, whether it was the tone and style of singing, or else the case that the form of song was, at that point, viewed with particular African-American connotations.

This contemporary impression of cultural style—the earliest we have of the sort—is significant. One might suspect that the atmosphere of Oberlin College at that time, the college being a center for abolitionism, helped engender what we might call an *ethnosympathetic hearing* of Black song.[9] Yet with the evidence we now have of the correlations between African-American work-songs and chanties, it is reasonable to suppose that the formal and stylistic similarities detected by Allen would have been palpable to other listeners.

"On Shanties"
—*Once a Week*, August 1868

The next article on our subject does not come until a decade later, after the chanty genre's practice had spread considerably, and this time in a British publication. The anonymously authored piece "On Shanties"—note the explicit use of the term—appeared in an August 1868 issue of *Once a Week*. Twenty titles are mentioned, some of whose verses are exemplified; seventeen were new in the published discourse and about five titles refer to songs unclear to us today.

The article is more systematic than those from a decade earlier. It is broken down between "capstan shanties" and "hauling shanties," several types of the latter being distinguished. And these are all differentiated from "songs sung in the foke's'ull, when Jack is taking his ease…"[10]

The author notes that the "mournful" and "wild" tunes of the songs were particular, yet their lyrics were not set and depended upon the invention of the singer. He says a bit about the various lyrical topics, noting for instance,

> There is an air of romance about California, the Brazils, and Mexico, that has a peculiar charm for Jack, and has made them the subject of many a favourite shanty, as *Rio Grande, Valparaiso, Round the Horn,* and *Santa Anna.*[11]

The *Once a Week* article was followed by another anonymous article in a British publication, "Sailors' Shanties and Sea Songs," in a December 1869 issue of *Chambers's Journal.* This one became ground zero for several later narratives. This is all the more significant in that very little if anything in the 1869 article is original. Unless this is the same author writing for the *Once a Week* piece, we must conclude that most of it was plagiarized from it. Material also seems to have been lifted from the 1858 *Atlantic Monthly* piece. The *Chambers's Journal* author takes the very same "Haul on the Bowline" anecdote of a "genuine sea-song" event, but turns the "English second-mate" into a Yankee (although, puzzlingly, the caricatured pronunciation of this officer still drops the "h" from the start of words). An even closer reading suggests that this author misunderstood some of the information lifted from the earlier pieces. There is the possibility that the *Chambers's* author had some knowledge of chanties, but that he chose to use all the material from earlier writing and only to tweak a few points. It is unfortunate then to find that this article, which gave the *Oxford English Dictionary* its first source for "shanty,"[12] was so flawed and unoriginal.

> *These songs produce the most*
> *singular effect upon the negroes…*
> —E. Kellogg, 1869

Among contemporary observers, Reverend Elijah Kellogg (1813–1901), while not writing quite so expressly about chanties, worked much information on them into his fiction works *The Ark of Elm Island* (1869) and *A Strong Arm and a Mother's Blessing* (1881). Kellogg appears to have based his information on personal experience of chanty-singing in earlier days. Born in Portland, Maine, Kellogg went to sea for three years as a boy ca. 1828–31.[13] He continued his interest in sailing while a student at Bowdoin College (1836–40), and later became pastor of the Mariners' Church and chaplain of the Sailors' Home in Boston, 1854–1866.[14] One may conjecture that his main experience with sailor worksongs—though he does not refer to them as chanties—occurred in the 1830s through the early 1850s. Making much of African-American chanty-singing, Kellogg speaks of "the natural disposition of the negro to sing when at work."[15] With this in mind, he notes a supposed special knack of many Black sailors with regards to chanty-singing.

> The songs of the negro seamen generally refer to their labor—hoisting or stowing molasses, or screwing cotton, which is severe labor, where unity of effort is of the first importance; and here the negro's accurate ear renders them most effective, and they will accomplish more, with less fatigue to themselves, than white men. No matter how many of them are on a rope, their pull tallies precisely with the time of the song, and they will put in the queerest quirks and quavers, but all in time. Perhaps there may be one negro in a million who has no idea of time. If such a one gets hold of the rope, and makes a false pull, it affects them as much as a false note would a well-drilled choir.[16]

Moreover, he remarks,

> These songs produce the most singular effect upon the negroes, insomuch that they seem hardly conscious of fatigue, even while exerting themselves to the utmost. Wages have been paid to a negro for merely singing when a large cargo of molasses was to be discharged in a hurry, the extra labor which he excited the rest to perform being considered as more than an equivalent for his wages, while it prevented a rival from obtaining his services.[17]

Within the narrative of his story, Kellogg inserts what we may suppose to be a more or less true observation from "many years ago" in Portland. Eight Black men were hoisting molasses aboard a brig, while singing. A white-collar Black employee came along and, hearing the song, could not resist stripping off his fine work clothes and joining in.[18] The extreme characterization of Black men as incorrigibly rhythmic and uncontrollably affected by song would be a difficult stereotype to justify today, but it speaks to the connotations of Blackness that chanties must have held for some early Euro-American observers.

In *The Ark of Elm Island*, Kellogg goes on to claim that, years later when a winch was introduced for the task of loading, Black men abandoned this labor because working a winch was not conducive of singing.[19] No doubt there was was more to situation than that! However, Kellogg uses that aspect rhetorically to emphasize again his association between Black laborers and work-singing. In his later work, Kellogg elaborates on his understanding, in effect making the profound claim that chanty-singing was a key mitigating factor determining the course of maritime commerce in Portland.

> The importance of the negro stevedores and seamen gradually diminished with the decay of the West India trade. But the first severe blow was inflicted in 1833, when the brig Oscar, belonging to Jacob Knight, a prominent West India merchant, came into Boston with a cargo of molasses. Mr. Knight took his blacks and went to Boston to discharge the vessel, and bring her back to Portland. He took a large crew of the smartest negroes, first-rate hoisters and singers, with the tackles and other gear, and Robert Craig for leading singer, with the two Shapleigh's, Isaiah Thomas, Young, Jere Brown, and Stewart, a man of enormous bulk and lungs in proportion...

> ...In the mean time Knight went among the shipping, and found cargoes there were with a winch, that this required less men, and more work could be done in the same time for less money. He therefore bought a winch (windlass turned by cranks) and brought it home in the brig. The negroes would have nothing to do with it, because they could have no song, for this machine did not admit of it. There was neither poetry, music, nor pleasant associations connected with turning a crank, and the Irish filled their places; the lumber was cut off; the negroes gradually disappeared and sought other employments, and the entire course of trade changed.[20]

Although the chanty-singing scenes elsewhere in Kellogg's *Ark* are anachronistic (being set in the eighteenth century), he makes it a point to emphasize the role of Black seamen. There is a scene in which an American and an English ship are racing each other to warp into dock. The captain of the English ship forbids his crew from singing, but the American crew, aided by its Black singers, works harder at the windlass.

> At intervals they would unite in one universal shout on the double chorus. Then Isaiah, bringing the flat of his foot down to advertise them of what was coming, came out on the word "ha-a" with a guttural so purely African, that the negroes would jump from the deck.[21]

The American ship ends up pulling far ahead of her competition. In all, *The Ark of Elm Island* contains texts of eight chanties and *A Strong Arm* contains five, with a characteristically ad-libbed type of verse and most of which are written in a "Black" dialect.

Another fiction writer with some fascination for, and likely some direct knowledge of chanties was Horace Elisha Scudder (1838–1902), of Boston. As an editor of and contributor to periodicals, including *The Riverside Magazine for Young People* (1867–70), he may have been responsible for unsigned stories that included original information on chanties. The author of an April 1868 article, "Sailors' Songs," in *The Riverside Magazine* presented early complete texts for "Shenandoah" and "Heave Away, My Johnnies," which he claimed to have learned on a recent Atlantic voyage.[22] Published prior to the important 1868 *Once a Week* article, this piece uses the term "chanty," being perhaps the first expositional publication to do so.[23] Another unsigned *Riverside* story from September 1870 sets the texts for "Whiskey Johnny" and "Haul Away Joe" on a ship leaving New York.[24] In one of Scudder's signed stories from 1879, he included four chanties, two of which compare well with the forms in the 1868 issue of *Riverside*.[25] I believe the inclusion of chanties in literary works such as these informed other literary authors who would go on to utilize chanties for color in their works. While perhaps seeming unremarkable, it is the early appearance (1860s–70s) of these works that makes them significant. For starting in the 1890s especially, writers would make it more common to quote familiar chanties, though their forms were often contrived or drawn from prior publications.

> *...he is sometimes allowed to spare his own exertions*
> *and reserve all his energies for the inspiriting shanty*
> —R. C. Adams, 1879

A father-son pair of Americans contributed significant discourse on chanties during the 1870s. The younger was Captain Robert Chamblet Adams, whose experiences on at least two vessels in the second half of the 1860s informed his knowledge of chanties. One was the barque *Rocket*, and the other was the ship *Dublin* that sailed from Boston, via Richmond, Virginia, to Genoa. In the latter case the crewmembers were all Black men who "made the decks ring with their songs." R. C. Adams writes of chanties first in an April 1876 magazine article, "Sailors' Songs." Not calling the songs "shanties" (yet using the term shantyman in reference to the song-leader[26]), he refers to thirteen familiar items, many for which a sample text is given. Notably, tunes, albeit with faulty rhythmic notation, are given for many items. This makes the article the earliest *extensive* record of chanty tunes. Also significant is Adams' indication of the syllables on which the "pulls" would occur. The younger R. C. Adams' later-published narrative of his voyages in *On Board the Rocket* (1879) is interspersed with four chanties of the Black crew. At the end of this volume he reprints the content of the "Sailors' Songs" article nearly verbatim save for a few additional sentences. In one of these additions, he at last refers to a "shanty" distinctly.[27]

Structurally, Adams distinguishes first those "sentimental songs sung in the forecastle, or on the deck in the leisure hours of the dog-watch, when the crew assemble around the fore-hatch to indulge in yarns and music,"[28] of which he informs us,

> Dibdin's songs, which the orthodox sailor of the last half century was supposed to adhere to as closely as the Scotch Presbyterian to his Psalter, are falling into disuse, and the negro melodies and the popular shore songs of the day are now most frequently heard.[29]

He goes on tell us of the "working songs," which he originally divides into the three sets corresponding to "those used where a few strong pulls are needed," "long hoists," and "those used at the pumps, capstan and windlass, where continuous force is applied"— along with the possibility that the repertoire of the last two categories overlap somewhat.[30] As such, he reinforces the task-based organization of the 1868 *Once a Week* article and sets a typical pattern for later authors. Along with the texts and brief commentary on their content, Adams informs us that the texts were often of little coherence and should be managed creatively by the chantyman. Indeed,

> A good shantyman is highly prized, both by officers and crew. His leadership saves many a dry pull, and his vocal effort is believed to secure so much physical force, that he is sometimes allowed to spare his own exertions and reserve all his energies for the inspiriting shanty.[31]

Adams polishes up his discussion with a statement on "the unnameable and unearthly howls and yells that characterize the true sailor, which are only acquired by years of sea service." Like few other authors, he gives specific examples of these forms, from "the continuous running solo…accompanying the hand-over-hand hoisting of jibs and staysails" to "short 'swigs' at the halyards," to "the more measured 'singing out,' for the long and regular pulls at the 'braces.'"[32]

R. C. Adams' father, Reverend Nehemiah Adams, accompanied him on a voyage (undertaken for his "health") in the ship *Golden Fleece*, from Boston to

San Francisco and Hong Kong, 1869–70. In the travelogue *A Voyage Around the World* (1871), the elder Adams offered five chanties that correspond to the son's later-published work. Nehemiah Adams speaks of a "shanty man" ("as they call him, solo singer"),[33] but not of "shanties"—just as his son did not do until 1879. And yet, his discourse suggests he may have seen either the 1868 *Once a Week* or 1869 *Chambers's Journal* articles (which do refer to "shanties"). A bit of the same is suggested by the details in R. C. Adams's book, particularly in the effort to classify song types and their purposes, suggesting that although R. C. Adams' work is probably original with respect to the repertoire forms it provides, Adams' ideas about how to present and describe chanties had been shaped according to a budding discourse on the topic.

We may add to this bunch of 1870s expositions J. Grey Jewell's *Among Our Sailors* (1874). It includes a section on "Sailors' Songs" in American vessels, the experience with which Jewell gained as a passenger who frequently joined in or observed the work. He found simply that sailors "have certain words and tunes for certain work,"[34] and of these he gives five original texts of familiar chanties. Interestingly, Jewell completes the leap started by the *Oberlin Monthly* author.

> When hauling taut the weather main-brace, they sing a perversion of the old negro melody, "Hey, Jim along, Jim along, Josey!" but the sailors put it—
>
> "Way, haul away—haul away, Josey—
> Way, haul away—haul away, Joe!"[35]

This is to say: A contemporary observer of the chanty genre in ships, well assimilated into Anglo culture, recognized its affinity to songs in African-American style. There was no effort to imagine this song, at least, as a direct descendant of English heritage.

> *...we owe the sailors' working song*
> *as we now possess it to the Americans.*
> -W. C. Russell, 1889

It may be of interest that up through the 1870s, the seeming heyday of chanty practice, most of this original literature—that which I describe as conscious writing on chanties—had been from American perspectives. In the 1880s, however, we get numerous statements from a British literary man with sailing experience. W. Clark Russell (1844–1911), born in New York to English parents, later to settle in London, spent the early part of his life sailing in British merchant ships, 1858–66. Beginning with one of his stories from 1875, he inserts a text that resembles "Blow, Boys, Blow."[36] Russell goes further in *Sailors' Language* (1883), mentioning (some version of) titles for "Santiana," "Across the Western Ocean," "Run, Let the Bulgine, Run," "Whiskey, Johnny," "Black Ball Line," and "Time for us to go."[37] The last of these being one of Dana's chanties now unclear to us (perhaps belonging to an earlier repertoire of songs overwritten by more familiar chanties) raises the question of whether Russell actually knew it; the others are plausibly attributable to his experience. In another story from the same year, he drops some of these same titles, plus "Haul the Bowline."[38] In 1888, and amongst other contemporary writing on the subject, Russell wrote an article in part dedicated to the subject.[39] The chanties he names here include those he had already given, plus "Rio Grande" and more from Dana; none are particularly remarkable, nor is his by-then-familiar explanation of the different work types.

What *is* notable in Russell's work is his venture to speculate on the origins of the genre. Russell notes that he could not find mention of chanties in older British accounts, and concludes they may be American in origin, despite his possible bias as a British sailor and author.

> It would be interesting to know when and by whom the working song was first introduced into the British Merchant Service. In old books of voyages no reference whatever is made to it. There is not a sentence in the collections from Hakluyt down to Burney to indicate that when the early sailors pushed at handspikes or dragged upon the rigging they animated their labours with songs and choruses. I have some acquaintance with the volumes of Shelvocke, Funnell, and other marine writers of the last century, but though many of them, such as Ringrose, Dumpier, Cooke, Snelgrave, and particularly Woodes Rogers, enter very closely into the details of the shipboard work of their time, they are to a man silent on this question of singing. It is for this reason that I would attribute the origin of the practice to the Americans.[40]

Having reasoned on lack of British-based evidence that the chanties must be American, Russell cites the lyrics of chanties as positive evidence suggesting American origins.

> If most of the forecastle melodies still current at sea be not the composition of Yankees, the words, at all events, are sufficiently tinctured by American sentiment to render my conjecture plausible. The titles of many of these working songs have a strong flavour of Boston and New

York about them...scores more of a like kind, all of them working songs...are racy in air and words of the soil of the States.[41]

By the time of one of his 1889 works, Russell felt confident to say that there was "no landsman who needs to be told" that sailors sing chanties,[42] which brings us to the period when non-mariners, at least in Britain, had become broadly aware of the genre's existence. Russell also tells us that at that time, despite steam power, the singing of chanties was still current, albeit on the wane.

> To be sure in these days steam and patent machinery have diminished something of the obligation of these chants. A donkey engine does its work without a chorus; it needs not a fiddler to set a steam capstan revolving. But the manual windlass is still plentiful, the capstan bar of our forefathers is not yet out of date, though the single topsail is halved there is yet the upper yard to masthead; and these, with a hundred other jobs to be done aboard a sailing ship, keep the sailors' sea-song actively current.[43]

At this juncture of mainstream awareness, Russell saw fit to add to his theory on the American origin—or at least adaptation—of chanties, including the idea that chanties are not older than the nineteenth century.

> I think it may be taken that we owe the sailors' working song as we now possess it to the Americans. How far do these songs date back? I doubt if the most ancient amongst them is much older than the century. ...The working song then is peculiar to the Merchant Service, but one may hunt through the old chronicles without encountering a suggestion of its existence prior to American independence and to the establishment of a Yankee marine. It is at least certain that the flavour of many of these songs is distinctly Transatlantic. The melodies it might be impossible to trace. Just as "Yankee Doodle" is an old English air Americanized by the inspirations of the Yankee poet, so there may be many an old tune that owed its existence to British brains appropriated by the Boston and New York lyrists, and fitted to words so racy of the soil as to render the whole production as entirely Yankee to the fancy as are the stripes and stars or the cotton white canvas of the ships of the States.[44]

If this was not enough, in his 1892 work Russell put his American origins of chanties idea down in an even more positive fashion. He declares that while forecastle songs were British, chanties were American.

[Americans] invented the double topsail yards; they invented the "chanty," the inspiring choruses of the windlass and the capstan... they were the first to lighten the sailor's labor by bidding him lift up his voice when he hove or shoved; they imported into their commercial marine fifty useful time- and labor-saving ingenuities, all which we on our side, blind with the scaly salt of centimes of dogged seagoing, were very slow to see, to apprehend, and to apply.[45]

Russell's work takes us to the atmosphere of awareness characterizing the 1890s, but we must yet go back to note some of the other 1880s material from before when this was the case.

Undoubtedly many sailor songs have a negro origin.
—W. L. Alden, 1882

Arguably the most important writing on chanties of this decade, both for its completeness and later influence, was the journalist William L. Alden's (1837–1908) "Sailors' Songs," in a July 1882 issue of *Harper's*. Most of the eighteen chanties he mentions are given with lyrics and, unlike few before (cf. R. C. Adams, 1879), with music notation. It is unknown where Alden learned the songs; being based in New York, one supposes he may have heard them as a passenger on ship or interviewed local sailors. His talk of chanties already contains notes of nostalgia for a dying genre. Russell's comments above notwithstanding, Alden subscribed to the idea that would later become very popular—that steam power, in killing off the traditional sailing art, had also killed off chanty-singing.[46] He writes: "The 'shanty-man'—the chorister of the old packet ship—has left no successors."[47] We need not take this literally, though it is enough to flag an issue: most observations of chanty-singing by deepwater sailors after the 1880s do not reflect the practice of the very historical genre about which they hoped to inform. Alden was among the last to write about this genre while it was still practiced as such, and those that follow mediated through memory.

In the piece, Alden elaborates on the classification of chanties with more details than had been done previously. And he explains the form of the different types of songs and how they were put together:

All sailor songs consist of one or more lines sung by the shanty-man alone, and one or two lines sung by the men in chorus. Windlass songs always have two choruses, while pulling songs should have but one. The choruses are invariable. They are the fixed and determinating quantities of each song, while the lines sung by the shanty-man were left in a measure to his discretion. It is true that custom wedded certain lines to certain songs, but the shanty-man was always at liberty to improvise at his own pleasure.[48]

The discussion includes the explanation of the grand chorus, and how this may distinguish the heaving shanties. Alden makes important notes about the style of singing. Remarkably, his opinions on style lead him to compare chanties to Black songs—both vernacular songs and minstrel songs, which he evidently believed to be cut from the same cloth.

The old sailor songs had a peculiar individuality. They were barbaric in their wild melody. The only songs that in any way resemble them in character are "Dixie," and two or three other so-called negro songs by the same writer. This man, known in the minstrel profession as "Old [Dan] Emmett," caught the true spirit of the African melodies—the lawless, half-mournful, half-exulting songs of the Kroomen. These and the sailor songs could never have been the songs of civilized men. They breathe the wild freedom of the jungle, and are as elusive as the furrow left by a ship on the trackless ocean.[49]

These observations lead Alden further to conclude that many chanties had their origins in Black music. He is the first discussant to connect them directly to cotton-stowing songs. And while he believes "certain" songs were English, he qualifies the idea by saying that those were an older layer of songs, offering the example of "Cheerly Man"—a song which other evidence does indeed suggest was one of the few from and earlier style of work-song that preceded the chanties that had come to flourish in his time.

Undoubtedly many sailor songs have a negro origin. They are the reminiscences of melodies sung by negroes stowing cotton in the holds of ships in Southern ports. The "shanty-men," those bards of the forecastle, have preserved to some extent the meaningless words of negro choruses, and have modified the melodies so as to fit them for salt-water purposes. Certain other songs were unmistakably the work of English sailors of an uncertain but very remote period. Of these the once famous "Cheerly, men," is a typical specimen. They were, however, frowned upon on board American ships because of their English origin...[50]

Alden's work was quite influential, yet only until the point where, as will be shown, its ideas were replaced by other narratives. One notes his characterization of certain songs and the genre in general in following works of the nineteenth century though, as will be seen, many authors of the early twentieth century seem to have missed the article in their research. The effect was that even "landsmen" without the sea experience of hearing chanties nonetheless acquired the notable idea of this contemporary observer: that there was an African-American connection.

To summarize this first layer of discourse: we see descriptions of chanties, during their heyday, mostly from the experiences and observations of Americans. All are clear about such things as the exclusivity of chanties as work-songs and among merchant sailors. There is no attempt to work foc'sle material into the canon. The authors established a way of presenting chanties according to the working tasks they would accompany, and underscored their necessity to a sailor's job. Chanties being a contemporary fact of life, there was little reflection on where chanties came from. However, the authors who did address the idea specifically note the similarity with and or origin in African-American songs (in the case of American writers) or just the origin in America (in the case of the British writer, Russell). Otherwise they distinguished chanties in terms of their style from familiar types of Euro-American singing. Being the voices of people most contemporaneous to the era of chanty-singing, we can take their impressions as having considerable value, even if few based their comments in historical research. Moreover, there having been little in writing prior about chanties, there is not much that can be called derivative; their comments were fairly independent testimonies of what was going on during the active period of chanty-singing. Nonetheless, one can see a semblance of common discourse beginning to form, in such gestures as distinguishing chanties from sailors' leisure songs and in classifying chanties by task, and through the gradual acceptance of a term for the genre and upon which to hang these discussions.

Key works

1858   [Unknown], "Songs of the Sea," *Atlantic Monthly* (Boston)

1858   Allen, "Songs of the Sailor," *Oberlin Students' Monthly*

1868   [Scudder?], "Sailors' Songs," *Riverside Magazine* (New York)

1868   [Unknown], "On Shanties," *Once a Week* (London)

1869   Kellogg, *The Ark of Elm Island* (Boston)

1869   [Unknown], "Sailors' Shanties and Sea Songs," *Chambers's Journal* (London)

1870   [Scudder?], "Shipmate Will Brown," *Riverside Magazine*

1871   N. Adams, *A Voyage Around the World* (Boston)

1874   Jewell, *Among Our Sailors* (New York)

1875   Russell, *John Holdsworth: Chief Mate* (London)

1876   R. C. Adams, "Sailors' Songs," *New Dominion Monthly* (Montreal)

1879   R. C. Adams, *On Board the Rocket* (Boston)

1879   Scudder, *The Bodleys on Wheels* (Boston)

1880   Kellogg, *A Strong Arm and a Mother's Blessing* (Boston)

1882   Alden, "Sailors' Songs," *Harper's* (New York)

1883   Russell, *Sailors' Language* (London)

1883   Russell, "Jack's Courtship," *Longman's Magazine* (London)

1888   Russell, "The Old Naval Song," *Longman's Magazine*

1889   Russell, *The Romance of Jenny Harlowe* (London)

1892   Russell, "A Claim for American Literature," *The North American Review* (New York)

Notes for chapter 1

1   That sailors did use the term "chanty" (i.e. in whatever spelling) in some quarters, by the late 1850s, is confirmed. In his journal while working aboard the whaleship *Atkins Adams* out of Fairhaven, Mass., 1858–9, W. A. Abbe mentions "shanties" several times.

2   "Songs of the Sea," *Atlantic Monthly* 2.9 (1858): 153.

3   Ibid., 154.

4   Isaac Allen, "Songs of the Sailor," *Oberlin Students' Monthly* 1.2 (1858): 46.

5   Ibid., 48.

6   Ibid., 48.

7   Ibid., 49.

8   A dating of 1840 or earlier for "Jim Along Josey" is in evidence from the Firth & Hall sheet music edition. See: Dale Cockrell, *Demons of Disorder: Early Blackface Minstrels and Their World* (Cambridge: Cambridge University Press, 1997), 5.

9   I allude to Jon Cruz's use of "ethnosympathy" to refer to what he identifies as a turn, in the mid-nineteenth century, towards interest in the inner world of human subjects. *Culture on the Margins: The Black Spiritual and the Rise of American Cultural Interpretation* (Princeton, NJ: Princeton University Press, 1999), 3.

10   "On Shanties," *Once A Week* 31 (1868): 93.

11 Ibid., 92.

12 "Shanty," in *A New English Dictionary on Historical Principles*, Vol. 8, part 2, ed. James A. H. Murray, Henry Bradley, and William A. Craigie (Oxford: Clarendon Press, 1914), 626.

13 Wilmot Brookings Mitchell, ed., *Elijah Kellogg: The Man and his Work* (Boston: Lee and Shepard, 1903), 51.

14 Ibid., 74.

15 Elijah Kellogg, *The Ark of Elm Island* (Boston: Lee and Shepard, 1869), 123.

16 Ibid., 124–5.

17 Ibid., 125.

18 Ibid., 125–7.

19 Ibid., 127.

20 Elijah Kellogg, *A Strong Arm and a Mother's Blessing* (Boston: Lee and Shepard, 1880), 197.

21 Kellogg, Ark, 129–30.

22 I am indebted to Jonathan Lighter for pointing out this source.

23 "Sailors' Songs," *The Riverside Magazine for Young People* 2.16 (1868): 185. If not from personal experience, the Riverside article's author may have read "chanty" (with the same spelling) in another recent Boston-based publication, George Edward Clark, *Seven Years of a Sailor's Life* (Boston: Adams), 1867.

24 "Shipmate Will Brown," *The Riverside Magazine for Young People* 4.45 (1870): 403–4.

25 Horace Elisha Scudder, *The Bodleys on Wheels* (Boston: Houghton, Osgood and Co., 1879).

26 Robert Chamblet Adams, "Sailors' Songs," *New Dominion Monthly*, April 1876, 259, 260.

27 Robert Chamblet Adams, *On Board the Rocket* (Boston: D. Lothrop, 1879), 311.

28 Ibid., 309–10.

29 Ibid., 310.

30 Ibid., 310–20.

31 Ibid., 311.

32 Ibid., 322.

33 Nehemiah Adams, *A Voyage Around the World* (Boston: Henry Hoyt, 1871), 23.

34 J. Grey Jewell, *Among Our Sailors* (New York: Harper & Brothers, 1874), 187.

35 Ibid., 188.

36 W. Clark Russell, *John Holdsworth: Chief Mate*, Vol. 1 (London: Sampson Low, Marston, Low & Searle, 1875), 19.

37 W. Clark Russell, *Sailors' Language* (London: Sampson Low, Marston, Searle, & Rivington, 1883), xi.

38 W. Clark Russell, "Jack's Courtship," *Longman's Magazine* 3 (1883): 25.

39 W. Clark Russell, "The Old Naval Song," *Longman's Magazine* 12 (1888).

40 Ibid., 181–2.

41 Ibid., 182.

42 W. Clark Russell, *Romance of Jenny Harlowe* (New York: D. Appleton, 1889), 336.

43 Ibid., 341.

44 Ibid., 338–9.

45 Russell, "A Claim for American Literature," *The North American Review* 433 (1892): 146.

46 See also a comment in 1884: "As steam has so largely superseded manual labor, the sea-songs with which sailors used to keep time when pulling and hauling in combined and simultaneous effort, are dying away in faint echoes, and soon they will only mingle with the discredited strains of the nearly forgotten mermaid." James McQuade, *The Cruise of the Montauk to Bermuda, the West Indies, and Florida* (New York: Thomas R. Knox, 1885), 102.

47 William Livingston Alden, "Sailors' Songs," *Harper's New Monthly Magazine*, July 1882, 281.

48 Ibid., 282.

49 Ibid., 281.

50 Ibid., 281–2.

II — EARLY COLLECTIONS (1880s–90s)

The end of the first era of discourse, as I have proposed it be circumscribed, coincided with the sharp decline in chanty practice aboard merchant ships. This situation would mean a shift in the perspective of writers, who were hearing chanties after their prime. In some cases, too, this meant writers were beginning to view them as something in need of salvaging. Hence, the idea of "collecting" material was formulated, in the response to modernity that would manifest academically as folklore studies. In this second layer we see the start of chanty anthologies. These created paradigms for later collections, and contributed material for later writers, both casual and conscious. The creation of molds and repetition of texts began to reshape the discursive "image" of chanties. Not only are they talked about in a new way, but their texts begin to appear more solidified and parts of the repertoire gain more emphasis than would have been the case in actual practice.

One could certainly consider the inventories of examples in R. C. Adams and Alden as "collections." However, they were not intended as such and the number of items in those cases is fairly small (under twenty). More importantly, the examples were just that—worked in to exemplify and to *explain* points regarding function and form. The earliest of what we might then recognize as a "collection" of chanties *for its own sake* was done in 1879, though its circulation was initially limited. This was the work of one George Haswell, who was a passenger on the S. S. *Parramatta* on a voyage from London to Sydney in the autumn of that year. Haswell collected ten chanties from the crew, noting their texts and tunes, and these were published in the ship's newspaper.[1] One could say that the honor goes to Haswell for being the first "chanty collector."

> *…the "Shanty-man" is relied upon to improvise, or to use*
> *some of the stock phrases which are well known to sailors.*
> —S. B. Luce, 1883

The next collection to be published—really a secondary compilation—appeared in a work by the American Admiral Stephen Bleeker Luce (1827–1917). *Naval Songs* (1883) was an anthology of entertainment songs; however, being related to sailor material, Luce included a discussion of chanties in its introduction. One presumes that Luce, a career naval officer and Academy instructor (he went on to become the first President of the Naval War College in Newport, Rhode Island), had some familiarity with most of the songs, if not the chanties. However, his lack of experience in merchant ships may explain why he chose to quote long passages from R. C. Adams' discussion. One will recall that by this point, Adams' book had been one of the only (along with Alden 1882) to include several chanties with *tunes*. Luce actually improves Adams' exposition by correcting the errors in notation.

Within Luce's anthology proper there are also two items that he labels "'Chantey' Song" and "Chanty Song" (respectively, "Blow the Man Down" and "Goodbye, Fare You Well"). His different spelling of "chantey"/"chanty" here, versus the use of Adams' "shanty" in the introduction, suggests derivation from another print source or at least experience with written discourse on the subject.

Naval Songs was published in a revised edition in 1902, which tweaks some of the chanty material, presumably in light of the significant publication on chanties in the two-decade interim. To begin with, Luce added a subtitle to his discussion of chanties: "Folk Songs of the Sea," bringing in a concept ("folk songs") that had no widespread familiarity at the time of his earlier edition. He explains why some chanties appear in the main text of his work, those being songs with longer developed and well-set narratives, whereas in most cases a chanty had,

> …but one or two lines peculiar to it; just sufficient, in fact, to identify it with its melody. After those are sung, the "Shanty-man" is relied upon to improvise, or to use some of the stock phrases which are well known to sailors.[2]

The exposition reveals the influence of a few recently published works, including Russell (above), (and below) L.A. Smith (1888), Lahee (1900), and Patterson (1900). Notable is the introduction of the organizational terms "short drag" and "long drag," which were not used by Adams (and perhaps inspired by Lahee).

The collection from this period that did the most to consolidate book-knowledge of chanties of the nineteenth century was Laura Alexandrine Smith's (?–1935) *The Music of the Waters* (1888). The volume's purpose was to present sea-and water-related songs of numerous national traditions of the world, among which Smith included a chapter called, "English and American 'Chanties;' or, Working Songs of the Sea." Though I cannot point to specific influence of it, Smith seems to have consulted W. Clark Russell,[3] for in one of his works of that time Russell alludes to "a lady writing to ask me to assist her in forming a collection of the sailors' working songs…"[4] As would be the case with many later "collections" this was a combination of both a compilation and original field collection. Without knowing that this was Smith's technique, however, it may look like Smith "collected" all of the material on chanties, and this is how I believe it was read by most subsequent authors.[5] Indeed, in her introduction, Smith makes much of her collecting activities, which explains the misunderstanding. We now know differently.

With the knowledge of prior works describe above, one can distinguish what was probably original and what was surely culled from earlier publications. Smith acknowledges her debt to the 1869 *Chambers's Journal* (whose incongruities she also repeats). Nine of her chanties come from that article, as well as much of the prose. Three probably come from the *Atlantic Monthly* article of 1858, and another, "Yeo Heave Ho," looks to have originated in an 1872 anthology of verse by English poet W. C. Bennett.[6] Two come from Leslie's *A Sea-Painter's Log* (1886).[7] Fourteen chanties, and again, much of the prose and ideas, came from Alden's article in *Harper's*. In fact, while we find Alden's ideas in later writers, these more often than not came via Smith's collection. Importantly, Smith reproduced all ten chanties from Haswell's shipboard newspaper article from *Parramatta*'s 1879 voyage.[8] These versions would have gone unknown otherwise, but in this case they were locked in to become the bases of many later interpretations. This leaves thirteen chanties (out of a total of about 55), which, in part due to not being able to tie them elsewhere, I believe were collected by Smith in the field. Mindful readers will also identify them by the fact that they all contain lyrics and tune, but that the lyrics are not placed directly beneath the notes in the musical notation.

Smith did her collecting in the Northeast of England, the Tyneside, interviewing retired sailors at the Sailors' Home. She does not give their names or their number. I must underscore that, unlike the writers of the previous layer of discourse, she did not hear the chanties in their working context. This was a time of decline in chanty use, as she says,

> Old tars tell us that the chanties are not what they were before steam became so universal: one added, on telling me this, "I'll tell you what it is, Miss, steamboats have not only taken the wind out of our sails, but they have taken the puff out of us too, and them as remembers ship-life as it was, will scarcely recognize it now-a-days.[9]

So while Smith provides some new details gathered from interviews, such as the idea that there were also songs for the work of holystoning the deck,[10] other aspects of chanty-singing she knew only from books—and frequently copied it directly from them.

Sailors' Songs or "Chanties"
—The title of the first anthology
published in Britain, 1887

There was another collection of sailor-songs published just before Smith's, although Smith would not have been aware of it in time (her introduction is dated June 1887). Yet this, also a British work, would become perhaps the most influential early collection of all: Davis and Tozer's *Sailors' Songs or "Chanties"* (published Aug. 1887). As a reference work it brings its own set of problems. For one, it is not written as a study of chanties, but rather provides a set of twenty-four songs designed to be performed, one can only imagine, as curious entertainment. The musical scores it contains are fleshed out with piano accompaniment, which, beyond being a convention of the time, raises the question of just who would have been interested to perform the songs at that time. Indeed, the use of "chanties" in quotes, as in Smith, confirms that the mainstream public was still not very familiar with the genre in the mid-1880s (whereas, we learned from Russell, they would become rapidly familiar by the end of that decade). What is in fact more notable is that, in order to provide "full" songs for novices to perform, texts of many connected verses are provided. Earlier publications rarely went beyond a single verse. When they did, reflecting what might have been really sung, the texts made no coherent whole. This does much to explain the lasting popular appeal of Davis and Tozer's work.

Captain Frederick J. Davis (?-1919) was in the merchant service for thirty years. While that may lead us to assume that he learned the songs firsthand, he says that he consulted members of Royal Navy and Mercantile Marine for the airs of some songs. Of the pair of editors, Davis was the sailor-authority, while Ferris Tozer was responsible for creating the musical settings. On the surface, it would appear (as many later writers would accept) that Davis was sharing authentic knowledge of chanties from his experience. And it is plausible that he was at least *familiar* with all of them. However, the form of the lyrics is suspicious. When we compare Davis texts to other documented versions of the same chanties, they often read as artificial or excessively polished in order to sound literary. Some of the seeming "nonsense" verse one finds in chanty texts as actually performed was rationalized to suit what was presumably the need of Davis' audience for rational texts with literal meanings. Close reading of Davis' texts and comparison to other sources of evidence suggests to me that after the first or second verse of each song, the rest of what was offered may have been entirely invented for publication. Even where verses sound plausibly authentic, there are as many cases where they seem unrealistic. For instance, the evidence now available suggests that the world "hilo" in chanties was something of indeterminate meaning (or with no verbal meaning at all) originating in African-American country songs. Yet in presenting "Tom's Gone to Ilo [Hilo]," Davis interprets it as the South American port of Ilo, which in turn may have inspired his line, "Hilo town is in Peru."[11] We may never know for sure if sailors themselves had made this "error," or if Davis contrived it in the moment, however, enough such suspect instances in the work point to a heavy editorial hand. All this makes the work an unacceptable source for historical evidence of the forms of chanties.

A second edition of Davis and Tozer's work came out in 1890, quickly followed by a third in 1891.[12] These added twenty-six chanties to the work, bringing the count up to fifty songs of which the editors acknowledge their debt to L. A. Smith. In fact, what they did was take examples from Smith's collection—several of which really originate with Alden—and extrapolate new lyrics. Later on, at the height of a chanty-singing revival among landsmen, Davis and Tozer's collection was issued again in a very slightly revised edition (1927). Its new forward invoked the idea of "folk music."[13]

This second layer of discourse was made possible by the increased recognition of chanties as a genre—a discrete topic of discussion. Writers used the material provided in the seminal articles to construct expansive collections of items. They were inspired by the sentiment of decline in chanty practice to gather together and present as much repertoire as possible, even if this meant taking many liberties with the repertoire. In some cases, their compilations, while motivated by preservation, did a certain amount of violence to the historical *understanding* of the genre by neglecting, confounding, or substituting individual visions of the genre's characteristics.

Key works

1883 Luce, *Naval Songs* (New York) [Revised, 1902]
1887 Davis and Tozer, *Sailors' Songs or "Chanties"* (London) [Enlarged, 1890, 1891]
1888 L. A. Smith, *The Music of the Waters* (London)

Notes for chapter 2

1 These were reproduced as *Ten Shanties Sung on the Australian Run 1879* (Antipodes Press, 1992).

2 Stephen Bleecker Luce, *Naval Songs*, second edition (New York: Wm. A. Pond, 1902), 219.

3 Ibid., 354.

4 Russell, *Jenny Harlowe*, 343. I am indebted to Jonathan Lighter for help in making this connection.

5 A recent (2013) BBC radio program about chanties ("The Drunken Sailor") dramatized a portion of Smith's text with the implication that she had gone along for a sailing voyage and collected chanties from sailors in that setting. The passage dramatized was in fact one that Smith had plagiarized from the 1858 *Atlantic Monthly* article, "Songs of the Sea."

6 See: William Cox Bennett, *Songs for Sailors* (London: Henry S. King, 1872), 15–6.

7 See: R. C. Leslie, *A Sea Painter's Log* (London: Chapman & Hall, 1886), 243–5.

8 Laura Alexandrine Smith, *The Music of the Waters* (London: Kegan, Paul, Trench & Co., 1888), 356.

9 Smith, *Music of the Waters*, 6.

10 Ibid., 7.

11 Frederick J. Davis and Ferris Tozer, *Sailors' Songs or "Chanties"*, third edition (London: Boosey, n.d. [1891]), 44.

12 I am indebted to Jonathan Lighter for his assistance in working out the editions.

13 Frederick J. Davis and Ferris Tozer, *Sailors' Songs or "Chanties"*, revised edition (London: Boosey, n.d. [1927]), 3.

The 1890s produced little original exposition on chanties, while innumerable literary works, on the other hand, began to take advantage of extant publications and the general awareness of the genre in order to paint pictures of maritime life. Writers like Rudyard Kipling, Charles Keeler, and Jack London seized upon chanties to evoke romance, nostalgia, and ruggedness.[1] But after the turn of the twentieth century came new expositional writing, albeit in a more nostalgic vein than seen in the previous century. The discourse at this time was divided between repetition of earlier narratives and the introduction of new ideas from the academic world of Folklore. The first of these orientations constitutes what I will call here the third layer of accumulated chanty discourse.

> *Now that the thing has gone by, we are alive to the*
> *fact that an old and romantic custom is dead or dying.*
> —H. C. Lahee, 1900

In 1900, while writing about British seafaring of the nineteenth century, historian Walter Jeffery (1861–1922) revived the common knowledge to that point, while voicing a narrative of the decline of the chanty genre.

> Occasionally, in the half-occupied East and West India docks, or in a foreign harbour, a chorus can still be heard from some merchantman weighing her anchor, but the steam winch is rapidly displacing the capstan and the windlass, and long before the end of the twentieth century chanty-singing will have become a memory.[2]

He asserts the authenticity of chanty repertoire as against the recent literary fancy.

> How different are these sea songs to the rubbish of the music halls! Girls in tights waving Union Jacks, and talking of "Shivering my timbers"—an expression unheard of in the annals of the sea—sing such rubbish as "Hilley hauley ho!" which is Greek in the ears of sailors, but is popularly supposed to be a sea song! Chanties are mainly composed for their usefulness, and not for the beauty of their music or the sense

of their verses; but there are songs that from their literary value are worthy of being sung anywhere.[3]

Probably having read works like Smith's (that reproduces Alden), this British-born author states the idea of the American or specifically African-American roots of the repertoire.

> Some of these songs go back to the time of the French War, but many of them have an American origin—the New Orleans cotton trade, when niggers were "screwing cotton all de day," having taught our sailors many good choruses. The American Civil War inspired several other songs...[4]

It is important to remember that the 19th-century writers maintained a perspective on chanties that held that the genre, in the main, was not older than the century and that it was distinctly American. Another historian of the nineteenth century, Arthur Hamilton Clark (1841–1922), was still saying the same ten years later when he included a retrospective view of chanties in his description of clipper ship sailing.

> These songs originated early in the nineteenth century, with the negro stevedores at Mobile and New Orleans, who sung them while screwing cotton bales into the holds of the American packet ships; this was where the packet sailors learned them. The words had a certain uncouth, fantastic meaning, evidently the product of undeveloped intelligence, but there was a wild, inspiring ring in the melodies, and, after a number of years, they became unconsciously influenced by the pungent, briny odor and surging roar and rhythm of the ocean, and howling gales at sea. Landsmen have tried in vain to imitate them; the result being no more like genuine sea songs than skimmed milk is like Jamaica rum.[5]

Such current ideas also informed musical history of the time. The volume *History of American Music* (1908) contains a chapter on "Patriotic and National Music."[6] In the description of chanties, the author takes the view that they were mostly born of Black cotton-stowers' songs.

> Most of the songs or chanties...of the American sailor of today are of negro origin, and were undoubtedly heard first in southern ports while the negroes were engaged in stowing the holds of the vessels with bales of cotton, while some few of them may be traced back to old English tunes...[7]

American publications continued to be informed by the presence of these narratives in their history of prior writing. For example, a National Broadcasting Company publication from 1944, evidently uninfluenced by the great shift in discourse in the 1910s and beyond, includes this note:

> With his gift for rhythmic song, the Negro proved to be an excellent shanty singer. Many shanties were originated by the Negro stevedores who loaded cotton on ships in the Gulf ports. A famous shanty which was taken over by sailors from these Negro stevedores is "Roll the Cotton Down."[8]

Yet we are getting ahead of the chronology. In fact, these two themes, the demise of chanties and their link to Black labor (especially cotton-stowing) were frequently found throughout this layer of discourse. The nostalgia engendered by the former, it might be argued, would contribute to the eventual neglect of the latter in the discourse of White authors.

Back at the turn of the twentieth century, American music historian H. C. Lahee, writing for the Boston Seaman's Friend Society, declared chanties "a thing of the past."[9] Acknowledging the irony of the contemporary interest he provides an excellent summary of the state of writing to that point.

> Now that the thing has gone by, we are alive to the fact that an old and romantic custom is dead or dying. Its rope is rapidly running through the block, and unless some one puts an overhand knot in the end, it will soon unreeve itself and be lost forever. During the past twenty years there have been a few magazine articles on the subject, one or two collections of chanteys in book form, and several allusions to the custom in various novels. Previous to that time it is not easy to find much allusion to the subject in literature. Not many knights of the pen went to sea, and of the few who did, scarcely any took notice of a custom which was as much a matter of course among sailors as going to the galley with a hookpot at seven bells. I do not mean to say that there is nothing on the subject, for I have found several allusions, but they are few in comparison to the number of books about the sea, and this leads us to imagine that many sea novels have been written by people whose knowledge of the mighty deep and its strenuous life is as fictitious as the stuff they write about it. And some of them have written books which, although they may be admired from a purely literary point of view and please the business man and his family, would be considered in the forecastle as more funny than the comic papers.[10]

Most of the melodies are undoubtedly of English origin...
—H. P. Whitmarsh, 1903

Two decades after the last in that magazine, an article about chanties appeared in *Harper's*. Canadian-Welsh sailor (c. 1878–84) and writer Hubert Phelps Whitmarsh's (1863–1935) nostalgic piece of 1903 marks the new way of discussing them. It puts an emphasis on a maritime ethos that finds its resonance especially in an Anglo cultural frame. Whitmarsh uses the phrase "sea chanteys" which, though it does appear a few times earlier, was never used consistently or with quite such a firm sense of purpose. His article is full of banalities like "smack of old ocean" and "true nautical swing,"[11] starting off, for instance, with the claim that chanties "hark back to such a remote period that it is impossible to say when or whence they originated..."[12] It is possible that he does not mean that chanties as we know them "hark back" to such a remote period; he may have adopted the idea of a chanty as any maritime work-song that one might dig up—in which case this is also a notable shift in conception. This might explain why he repeats the ideas of cotton ports as a site of origination and some chanties bearing "ear-marks of negro singers,"[13] on one hand, while also saying,

> Most of the melodies are undoubtedly of English origin, though in many cases they have been influenced by contact with other nations. Thus we find a number of ancient airs set to words distinctly American...[14]

Compare Whitmarsh's assertion of "undoubted" English origin with earlier writers' assertions of "undoubted" African-American origin. While not being able to deny the Americanness of some songs, the credit for the songs is thus diffused. While earlier writers mentioned above cited the "plaintive" nature of chanties as a connection to Black song, Whitmarsh uses the same characteristic to compare chanties to all kinds of global music.

> ...in listening to the plaintive melodies like "Storm-along" and "The Lowlands," I have at times been reminded of a Gaelic psalm chant, such as is sung by the Scotch Highlander and their descendants in Cape Breton; and again, they have seemed akin to the weird recitative and chorus of the aboriginal Australian.[15]

If I may be permitted an argumentative question, it would be: just what is the point of this comparison? To cast such a wide net in grouping music that appears to the observer as "plaintive" and "weird" is almost postmodern in outlook. I believe this sort of vagueness, which would reemerge later in the century, dilutes the impression of earlier observers, grounded in direct experience, that what they heard as "plaintive" was something particularly African-American.

> *Since 1872 I have not heard a*
> *Shanty or Song worth the name.*
> —W. B. Whall, 1908

The tail end of this era of discourse was filled with some substantial publishing of memories from veteran sailors who had sung them earlier in life. All recognized the passing of chanty practice, and brought their expertise to the table in preserving what was remembered. Moreover, they contributed original material to the body of evidence and were not affected much by prior published material.

The first of these was James H. Williams (1864–1927), an African-American seaman of the mid-1870s through 1880s, from Massachusetts. In New York and writing for *The Independent* in 1909, he called the chantyman an "almost extinct functionary."[16] Chanties were "sung no more" and "hushed forever."[17] His article mentioned twenty-one chanties, with extended sample lyrics for most of them. Indeed, almost in the manner of a folklorist, Williams says he got the texts from two particular shipmates, Gary Owen and "Splitnose" Sweeney.

Another writer in this vein was Swedish-American Fred Buryeson, whose article "Sea Shanties" (note the phrase) was published in a San Francisco seamen's magazine in the same year. Buryeson had sailed for over thirty years under flags of many nations. The article, which included extended lyrics to twenty-two chanties, also stated that chanties had then gone out of use.[18] Buryeson's chanty texts may date from as early as 1872, when he first sailed in the American ship *Ivanhoe*.[19]

Up to this point the extended *expositions* on chanties by Britons had still been few. There was the anonymous *Once a Week* piece (1868, cannibalized by *Chambers's Journal*, 1869). There were Russell's observations (1870s–90s) that do not include details of songs. Then there was Davis and Tozer's unannotated and non-authoritative collection (1887ff.) and L. A. Smith's lay collecting work in the Northeast of England. The British voice was at this point magnified with the publications of Captain William Boultbee Whall (c. 1847–1917). Whall's sea career began in 1861, from which point, remarkably, he had already begun to "collect" chanties he heard. He tells us,

...these sailor songs and shanties struck me as worthy of preservation. During my eleven years in those ships I took down the words and music of these songs as they were actually sung by sailors, so that what I present here may be relied upon as the real thing.

Since 1872 I have not heard a shanty or song worth the name. Steam spoilt them. A younger generation of seamen took the place of the old sea dog...With the new generation true sea songs and shanties practically disappeared. Echoes of them, it is true, still exist, but that is all. The real thing has gone for ever.[20]

Steam was not the only thing that "spoilt" chanties, according to Whall. In the remains of sailing ships, there were still the "remains" of chanties,

...but the character has all gone out of them. It is absurd to suppose that Dutchmen or Dagos, who chiefly man our sailing ships now, can in any way truly appreciate our ancient, wild hooraw choruses.[21]

As the above passage indicates, Whall was no unbiased collector. It is clear throughout his text that he deemed only certain songs and ways of singing them to be legitimate and worthy of inclusion. For example, he claims that, "seamen who spent their time in cargo-carrying sailing ships never heard a *decent* Shanty,*" and condemns such renditions as "the veriest filth." By contrast, seamen in "passenger and troop ships" understood that their words were to be "decent."[22] It was in the latter cases only that Whall believed chanties "were sung to their proper words." Further, though Whall admits that a "good" chantyman would improvise beyond a set of what he called "regulation" (obligatory, fixed) verses, he states, in conflict with other evidence, that "most of the good ones had a story in verse that never varied..."[23] The effect of this bias on the outcome of his work is revealed in his comment:

It was in these vessels—and these only—that a collector of songs was wanted, and it was only in such vessels that such a collection could have been made.[24]

In addition, Whall's text reveals a prejudice against African-American songs and culture. He claims that,

The white seaman in smart ships seldom condescended to sing "nigger" songs...Some were better than others, but nearly all were of a poor class.[25]

Though Whall states his chanty material is uninfluenced by earlier publications— and this I believe to be true—he indicates that he had read a number of books on the subject. Thus it is what he says about the material, if not the material itself, that shows his influences. Indeed, he ventures to play the role of historian, speculating on chanty origins. Seizing the idea of a chanty as generic label that includes earlier eras of seafaring song, he cites passages in *The Complaynt of Scotland* (1549)—incorrectly dating it to 1450—as supposed evidence of Medieval English chanty-singing.[26] This puts him first in a line of many authors to do the same. As a matter of fact, he might be called the first collector to try to explain origins and dating before presenting each song—a paradigm followed by later authors and revival singers.

Whall first published his collected material anonymously in two 1906 magazine articles, in *The Nautical Magazine* and *Yachting Monthly*. When these were brought together in book form in November 1910 as *Ships, Sea Songs and Shanties*, it formed what might be considered the first modern-style chanty collection. Whall provides a few verses for each chanty (entertainment songs were also included), beneath tune notations. Being musically literate, it is possible that Whall notated the tunes himself; they are in good form. Whall's brother, however, a more skilled musician, composed piano accompaniments. A second edition (1912) and a third edition (1913) of the collection soon followed, expanded to include more songs, for a total of thirty-two chanties. The collection was expanded and reissued yet again for a fourth edition (1920), this time containing fourty-four chanties plus fragments. Most notably, the last added a section called "Nigger Songs," which Whall explains by saying,

> In previous editions I have only given one example of the purely nigger shanty— "Stand to your ground." But it seems to be the wish of some of my readers that I should go further afield.[27]

This implies that, due to his low regard for them, Whall had left out (or failed to collect) most chanties that he thought were of Black origin. It also implies that he did not believe much of the familiar chanty repertoire to be of Black origin *in any case*, since he did include many that, with today's evidence, one may connect to Black culture. This seems remarkable since, he admits, "Nigger shanties there were by the hundred."[28] Moreover, the fact that he excluded these chanties meant that he was excluding, indeed, still many of the well-known and popular items (e.g. "Sacramento," "Clear the Track," and "Jamboree"). In all, Whall's is a valuable collection for the originality of its material, yet it gives something of a misleading picture of the repertoire due to its selectiveness and its commentary.

*...the great majority of these tunes undoubtedly emanated
from the negroes of the Antilles and the Southern states...*

—F. Bullen, 1914

An excellent work for comparison to Whall's is one by a different London ex-seaman who appears to have lacked the former's prejudices. Frank T. Bullen (1857–1915) first went to sea in 1869 and quit in 1880, thus experiencing shipboard chanties in their glory. Unlike officers (captains) such as Davis and Whall, Bullen remained in the foc'sle as a chantyman "engaged in trades where Chanties were not only much used on board, but where many new ones were acquired in the harbours": "the West Indies and the Southern States of America."[29] Thirty years after first going to sea at the age of eleven, Bullen noted his initial encounters with local stevedores in Demerara singing chanties.[30] This evidently made such an impression that chanty-singing became a part of his own identity.

> Being possessed of a strong and melodious voice and a tenacious memory, Chanty singing early became a passion with me, and this resulted in my being invariably made Chantyman of each new vessel I sailed in, a function I performed until I finally reached the quarter-deck, when of course it ceased...[31]

When, in 1913, Bullen finally poured his knowledge into *Songs of Sea Labour*, he created an invaluable record of the repertoire of a chantyman from the days when the genre was at its height. He is refreshingly genuine; stating that chanties had no set words beyond the first one or two lines and their chorus, he refuses to print any lines beyond that. Perhaps even more boldly, he resists the tendency to mix in leisure songs (as Whall did—the "sea songs" portion). There was no reason, in fact, to present leisure songs and chanties together under one cover as "sailor songs."

> Another omission is that of Sea Songs. They are not Chanties, nor have they ever been used as such. Therefore they are out of place in a collection of Chanties...[32]

It was only begrudgingly that Bullen, persuaded by his collaborator that it would be a wise gesture not to "disappoint the majority of those interested" in such a book,[33] consented to include two "sea songs": "Spanish Ladies" and "Lowlands Low" (i.e. "The Golden Vanity"). Bullen's singing was transcribed for publication by W. F. Arnold, an academically trained musician. In all there are forty chanties with (in the custom of the time) piano accompaniment, making it the largest original collection yet.[34] It is the concentrated, core practical repertoire of a chantyman. At odds with what we are led to believe from Whall, Bullen says that,

> ...the great majority of these tunes undoubtedly emanated from the negroes of the Antilles and the Southern states, a most tuneful race if ever there was one, men moreover who seemed unable to pick up a ropeyarn without a song...[35]

Again: "undoubtedly"! My own assessment of the origins of each chanty in Bullen's collections supports his claim.

Bullen's opinion was shaped by the specific conditions under which he learned chanties. He relates an anecdote of when he first learned "Mudder Dinah":

> We were discharging general cargo in the Demerara River off George-town, and all the wonder I could spare, being a first voyage laddie, was given to the amazing negroes who, not content with flinging their bodies about as they hove at the winch, sang as if their lives depended upon maintaining the volume of sound at the same time... I became most anxious to learn it, so I asked one of our two boat-boys to teach me...He set about his pleasant task at once but was very soon pulled up by his mate who demanded in indignant tones what he meant by teaching "dat buckra chile" [i.e. that White boy] dem rude words.[36]

For his claims about cultural origins Bullen had not only the weight of his experience with the style of these songs, but also the support of the musicologist Arnold. Arnold penned a two and one-half-page exposition on music of African-Americans, complete with an unexpectedly technical discussion of pentatonic scales, resting tones, and rhythmic devices, accompanied by the following justification:

> Seeing that the majority of the Chanties are Negroid in origin, perhaps a few remarks on Negro music will not be out of place here...[37]

While a few later writers acknowledged Bullen's work, it seems to have gone largely unread (if not unseen) or dismissed. What Bullen was saying about the origin of chanties, and what he was presenting—including lyrics and dialect forms that were unmistakably African-American—was really nothing that had not been voiced already in the nineteenth century. However, his work came well into the time after a newer layer of discourse had begun—one which marginalized African-American contributions and emphasized a British origin for and character of chanties. Thus, even the NAACP publication *The Crisis*, under the editorship of W. E. B. Dubois, took note of what must have seemed to be, to laypersons, an uncommon idea.

> According to Frank T. Bullen in London *Tit Bits*, the majority of chanties, sea-songs sung by sailors, come from the Negroes of the southern states, the crude songs being sung to lighten hours of labor.[38]

An important implication of the perspective displayed in *Songs of Sea Labour* is that, when Bullen was singing these songs as chantyman, he must have seen himself as a White man singing Black music. I do not imagine this is something many writers of the time wanted to envision.

As may well be imagined,
I cannot exactly recall all the original verses...
—J. Robinson, 1917

Something of an outlier time-wise, which might still be included in this layer, are the memories of chanties by a veteran sailor of the 1860s–70s, Captain John Robinson (c. 1845–1922). Robinson first went to sea at the age of thirteen around 1859; he spent 48 years at sea. He learned chanties on his first voyage, on the brigantine *Emily* to Sicily (especially from a sixty-year veteran of the sea named Will Halpin) and during two 1864 voyages from Sunderland to Chile (from a Dick Loveless). Robinson later joined the ship *France* of the National Steamship Company as an officer in 1873, and worked his way up through the ranks to Captain. Until 1907, he was "never three consecutive months on land."[39] One presumes that throughout this time, even though an officer, Robinson had some exposure to chanties.

The editor of a Minneapolis-based periodical, *The Bellman*, encountered Robinson and learned of his knowledge of chanties on a voyage some time before 1907. When the editor met Robinson years later, retired at his home in Watford (England), he urged him to write down the lyrics of chanties for publication. The *Bellman* editor also arranged for a musician to transcribe the melodies of Robinson's singing.[40] The result was a series of four articles published in July–August 1917 in the form of a semi-biographical narrative surrounding the presentation of chanty texts and their tunes with piano accompaniment. All together, the collected chanties in the series numbered thirty-three, and included a few "lime-juice" chanties that were supposed to be particular to British ships.[41]

Robinson's continuous experience, in first sail and then steam, gives some insight on the decline of chanties in ocean vessels. Steamships did not necessarily, or at least not entirely, kill the art.

> The advent of steamships and the use of steam power almost eliminated the chanty-man, but not quite, although his fate was sealed and certain. Even when steam-driven ships became almost universal, he still survived on the large North Atlantic liners, because, as the old packet ships were put out of commission, the crews, or "packet rats," swarmed on board the liners…[42]

He goes on to explain that "steam power was not to be used in making or taking in sail," and so these operations continued, and chanties were sung for them.

> …the chanty-man continued to exist, for a time, but his end was near. Early in the nineties the heavy yards were being abolished, as the speed of the ships increased, and in a few years the square-rigged merchant ship was a thing of the past. When the yards came down, the crews were reduced. Thus the song of the chanty-man was ended.[43]

Moreover, Robinson asserts, it was not just the replacement of sailing ships with steam that ended chanties, but also the replacement of the square-rigged ships by schooner-rigged ships (which lack yards to hoist), that contributed.[44]

While Robinson's collection is rather exciting as a record of experience, it appears not to be completely original. Robinson provides the following important disclaimer about the chanty texts:

> As may well be imagined, I cannot exactly recall all the original verses… In a crude way, however, I have endeavored to carry the spirit and sense of the originals into the words which I have written down.[45]

In order to supply the lyrics he could not remember, it seems that Robinson may have consulted some published sources. For example, his version of "Lowlands" has lyrics that might be considered out of character with other documented original versions, making it seem less like a traditional style and more like the fanciful text of Masefield (below).[46] The influence of reading is also evident in his ideas about origins. He takes a universal approach, speculating that there may have been chanties in 15th-century English ships[47]— here suggesting he read Whall's book. Robinson's statements reflect in some degree the influence of the speculative folklore approach of a layer of discourse that had become established by that time.

Similar in method and discursive style to Robinson, but later still in the chronology, is the writing of American sailor Frederick Pease Harlow. Harlow shipped out of Boston in December 1875 in the clipper ship *Akbar* bound to Australia and Java. He also visited Barbados in 1878, where he made some observations of local stevedores' chanties.[48] He shared around thirty chanties from his experience within an account of his Akbar experiences published in 1928, *The Making of a Sailor or Sea Life Aboard a Yankee Square-Rigger*. Though Harlow had enough material for a chanties-focused collection at that time, he was advised to hold off on publishing such a volume,[49] and additional chanty material did not see print until 1948.[50] It was only an excerpt, however, from a larger manuscript that was finally published, posthumously, as *Chanteying Aboard American Ships* (1962).

Harlow tells us that chanties were sung during his time in all square-riggers and even in brigs and topsail schooners (the implication being any vessel with yards to be hoisted), contributing to the overall impression that the 1870s represented the zenith of the genre.[51] Harlow's body of writing is rather exciting for this reason. However, the chanties within it are not a "pure" representation of what he heard sung at sea. Harlow's notes in the text indicate that before writing he had referenced Dana, L. A. Smith, Masefield, Whall, Lubbock (*Round the Horn Before the Mast*, 1902), Luce, A. H. Clark, Terry (below), Colcord (below), and Buryeson. Indeed, close reading reveals that some elements of these texts were mixed in with the versions of chanties he presents. He also presents items directly and with acknowledgment from William's 1909 article and from an unpublished source, Captain J. L. Botterill. Containing much original content, Harlow's *Chanteying Aboard American Ships* is now an indispensable desk reference for singers involved in the sea music revival; however, because its original content is seamlessly muddled with derivative material and because it was written from a first-person perspective so long after the events took place, it must be used with caution in scholarship.

Although it, too, appears much very late, in 1946—over four decades after I propose that this layer of discourse emerged—there is a last work to be considered in the literature of individuals chiefly remembering chanties across the divide. James T. Hatfield was a passenger on the barque *Ahkera*, from Pensacola, Florida to Nice, France, in 1886. Hatfield states that though he often traveled by sea again after that trip, he never again heard a chanty.[52] He recounted that the crew consisted entirely of Black men from Jamaica, among which several acted as chantyman. The set of their chanties remembered by Hatfield is valuable because he noted them when he heard them and, he asserted, just as he heard them. Hatfield's daughter, who organized her deceased father's data, notes, "He told me that he often requested them [the chanty-singers] to begin again and again until he could note the exact timing and melody."[53] Hatfield's daughter arranged the chanties her father collected for publication in the *Journal of American Folklore*. The set contains notable original variations of familiar items, along with some items that are not contained elsewhere.

To summarize this layer of discourse: This was the period during which the general use of chanties in merchant ships finally ceased. In the 1890s, just as chanties were starting to die, people began to find out what they were and take an interest. Yet with the turn of the century, the possibility of direct observation was increasingly rare, and the idea of methodically collecting songs through fieldwork (the next layer) had only begun. Therefore, writers either relied mainly upon ideas from older works, in the case of laypersons or, in the case of experienced sailors, on their memories. There was the sentiment of salvaging and preservation of the sailor's tradition. One also sees a split in perspective as to whether "chanties" belonged to African-America or "sea shanties" belonged to Britain. This era produced both substantial evidence from which to glean what chanties used to be like and fodder to be utilized by amateur enthusiasts.

Key works

1900 Jeffery, *A Century of Our Sea Story* (London)
1900 Patterson, "Sailors' Work Songs," *Good Words* (London)
1900 Lahee, "Sailors' Chanteys," *The Sea Breeze* (Boston)
1902 Lubbock, *Round the Horn Before the Mast* (London)
1903 Whitmarsh, "The Chantey-man," *Harper's* (New York)
1906 Bernard, "Sea Songs and Chanties," *The Nautical Magazine* (Glasgow)
1906 Whall, "Sea Melody—I," *The Nautical Magazine*
1906 Whall, "The Sea Shanty," *Yachting Monthly* (London)
1908 Whall, "Real Sea Songs," *The Nautical Magazine*
1909 Buryeson, "Sea Shanties," *Coast Seamen's Journal* (San Francisco)
1909 Williams, "The Sailors' 'Chanties'," *The Independent* (New York)
1910 Clark, *The Clipper Ship Era* (New York)
1910 Whall, *Ships, Sea Songs and Shanties* (Glasgow) [Enlarged, 1912, 1913, 1920].
1914 Bullen and Arnold, *Songs of Sea Labour (Chanties)* (London)
1917 Robinson, "Songs of the Chanty-Man," *The Bellman* (Minneapolis)
1928 Harlow, *The Making of a Sailor* (Salem, MA)
1946 Hatfield, "Some Nineteenth Century Shanties," *Journal of American Folklore* (New York)

1948   Harlow, "Chanteying Aboard American Ships" [excerpt], *The American Neptune* (Salem)

1962   Harlow, *Chanteying Aboard American Ships* (Barre, MA)

Notes for chapter 3

1   See e.g.: Rudyard Kipling, "The Last Chanty," *The Pall Mall Magazine* 1.1 (1893); Charles Keeler, *A Wanderer's Songs of the Sea* (San Francisco: A.M. Robertson, 1902); Jack London, *The Son of the Wolf: Tales of the Far North* (New York: Grosset and Dunlap, 1900), 210–1.

2   Walter Jeffery, *A Century of Our Sea Story* (London: John Murray, 1900), 165.

3   Ibid., 165.

4   Ibid., 164.

5   Arthur H. Clark, *The Clipper Ship Era* (New York and London: G.P. Putnam's Sons, 1910), 110.

6   W. L. Hubbard, ed., *History of American Music* (Toledo: Irving Squire, 1908), 133–5.

7   Ibid., 133.

8   NBC University of the Air, *Music of the New World: Handbook*. Vol. 3. (New York: Southern Music Company. 1944), 46.

9   Henry C. Lahee, "Sailors' Chanteys," *The Sea Breeze* 13.1 (1900): 13.

10 Ibid., 13.

11 H. Phelps Whitmarsh, "The Chantey-man," *Harper's Monthly Magazine*, January 1903, 320.

12 Ibid., 319.

13 Ibid., 319.

14 Ibid., 319.

15 Ibid., 319–20.

16 James H. Williams, "The Sailors' 'Chanties'," *The Independent*, July 8, 1909, 76.

17 Ibid., 76.

18 Fred H. Buryeson, "Sea Shanties," *Coast Seamen's Journal*, June 23, 1909, 1. I am indebted to the late George Salley for providing me early access to this source.

19 United States Merchant Marine Commission, *Report of the Merchant Marine Commission, Together with the Testimony Taken at the Hearings*, Vol. 1 (Washington: Government Printing Office, 1905), 212.

20 William Boultbee Whall, "Real Sea Songs," *The Nautical Magazine* 80.6 (1908): 548.

21 William Boultbee Whall, "Sea Melody," *The Nautical Magazine* 76.1 (1906): 29. In the issue of *The Nautical Magazine* immediately preceding one of Whall's articles, another British captain complained similarly that "simple melodies" of English sailors were, in 1906, "scarcely ever heard among the Hans and Antonio tribe [i.e. Germans and Italians] of the present day." D. H. Bernard, "Sea Songs and Chanties," *The Nautical Magazine* 75.6 (1906): 435.

22 William Boultbee Whall, *Ships, Sea Songs and Shanties*, third edition (Glasgow: J. Brown and Son, 1913), xii.

23 Ibid., xiii.

24 Ibid., xiii.

25 William Boultbee Whall, *Sea Songs and Shanties*, fourth edition (Glasgow: J. Brown and Son, 1920), 102.

26 Whall, *Ships, Sea Songs*, third edition, x.

27 Whall, *Sea Songs and Shanties*, fourth edition, 102.

28 Ibid., 102.

29 Frank T. Bullen and W. F. Arnold, *Songs of Sea Labour (Chanties)* (London: Swan, 1914), vi.

30 Frank T. Bullen, *The Log of a Sea-Waif* (New York: D. Appleton, 1899), 33–4.

31 Bullen and Arnold, *Songs of Sea Labour*, vi.

32 Ibid., xii.

33 Ibid., xvi.

34 Davis and Tozer's (1891) and Smith's (1888) works, although containing a slightly higher count, had borrowed much of their material from earlier works.

35 Bullen and Arnold, *Songs of Sea Labour*, xii.

36 Ibid., xiii.

37 Ibid., vii.

38 "Along the Color Line: Music and Art," *The Crisis* 8.6 (1914): 270.

39 John Robinson, "Half a Century at Sea," *The Bellman*, July 7, 1917, 10.

40 John Robinson, "Songs of the Chanty-Man: I," *The Bellman*, July 14, 1917, 10.

41 I imagine that these are the items that were associated with the trade with South America in later decades, like "Randy Dandy O," "Gals of Chile" ("Bangidero"), and "Slav Ho."

42 Robinson, "Songs of the Chanty-Man: I," 39.

43 Ibid., 39.

44 Ibid., 41.

45 Ibid., 38.

46 For the broader argument, see: Gibb Schreffler, "Twentieth Century Editors and the Re-envisioning of Chanties: A Case Study of 'Lowlands'," *The Nautilus* 5 (2014).

47 John Robinson, "Songs of the Chanty-Man: II," *The Bellman*, July 21, 1917, 70.

48 Frederick Pease Harlow, *Chanteying Aboard American Ships* (Mystic, CT: Mystic Seaport, 2004), 241–2.

49 Letter from George Francis Dow of Marine Research Society, Salem, to F. P. Harlow, 21 June 1928. G. W. Blunt White Library, Mystic Seaport Museum.

50 This chapter from a planned book was named with the title eventually given the entire manuscript, "Chanteying Aboard American Ships," and published in *The American Neptune* 8.2 (1948).

51 Harlow, *Chanteying*, 1.

52 James Taft Hatfield, "Some Nineteenth Century Shanties," *Journal of American Folklore* 59.232 (1946): 109.

53 Ibid., 109.

IV — THE EMERGENCE OF FOLKLORE STUDIES (1900S–1910S)

An early 20th-century turn in chanty discourse was characterized by the incorporation of concepts and methods from the growing field of Folklore. It began a few years into the start of the century, with the discussions of both professional scholars of folklore and lay writers who were influenced by early Folklore's concept of idealized "national" musics.[1] Whereas the 19th-century British writer Russell doubted any life of chanties in English culture before that century and before the introduction of American maritime innovations, turn of the 20th-century American writer Whitmarsh, we have seen, believed chanties to be "ancient airs" originally English. This near flip-flop was the product of a new discursive perspective.

Yet attempting to view chanties as a national music—a musical genre embedded with the long-developed traits and sensibilities of the *Volk* of a region—would be challenging. Some might think the main challenge lay in trying to ascribe a land area association with a genre supposedly developed "at sea," i.e. in between lands, or else to ascribe nationality to mixed, international crews. I do not believe it unreasonable to ascribe definite cultural (although not really "national") bases to the genre, nor do I believe that the "at sea" dimension makes it impossible to identify regions of origin; the genre might not even have been developed on water as much as on land. Rather, the issues with early folklorists attempting to see chanties as music of an ethnic nation were different. For one, this notion inclined scholars to look for certain essences to the exclusion of other characteristics and thus downplayed the "mixed" nature of the genre (something that would, perhaps, be over-corrected later in the century). This orientation also tended to ignore newer and "popular" influences in its search for ideal notions of "folk" music as something very old and inherent. Last, the frame of "national" music was limited to "folk" who appeared to be contiguous with the concept of the nation. Were the folk of the United States an offshoot of the English? Where did this leave other ethnic heritages of America? Did America have distinctive "folk" music at all?

Most important to note is that the writers in this discourse were not mainly historians. So while they had not seen the chanty genre in its prime, neither did they make much attempt to understand its past through historical references. Analysis of the currently-observed textual and musical forms—perhaps assumed to adequately represent the past—led to hasty inferences. And yet the goal was never much to say anything revealing about the chanty genre, but rather to use chanties to say something about folk-song. To writers in this vein, chanties were pre-established as "folk-songs," set within a people's tradition. They were not in need of critique or investigation, but rather in need of saving and canonizing.

I have never heard a pumping chanty...
—J. Masefield, 1906

Although British writers would come to characterize this layer, perhaps the first article on chanties by and oriented towards academic Folklore was by an American professor of English literature, Percy Adams Hutchison (1875–1952) of Harvard University. Writing about chanties for the *Journal of American Folklore* in 1906, Hutchison addresses the topic of "communal composition" in relation to English ballads, of which he thinks chanties are an example. Hutchison culls his texts from secondary sources (though he did also hear chanties as a passenger in earlier times), and uses them as supposed authentic examples to contrast with literary composition. A work of Kipling (a "chantie of art") is contrasted with "Goodbye Fare Ye Well," which Hutchison says is "a genuine capstan chantie," though we can notice it was taken from Davis and Tozer's collection.[2]

> Clearly, this chantie grew... That each line has been improvised to suit the exigencies of the moment is evident; the only necessitation one feels is in regard to the rhyme-word of the second solo-line. Conscious structure there is none, or almost none. Line could interchange with line, stanza with stanza, the whole could be longer or shorter, and the chantie would be no worse, and no better, structurally, than it is now. The whole is haphazard, inconsequential, and, excepting the refrain, absolutely spontaneous...[3]

> [...] Even the most primitive ballad we can bring forward has, by reason of generations of repetition, become a better piece of work, structurally, than we can expect any chantie to be.[4]

This idea of communal composition—for Hutchison does not bother to give the name of his source—is the essence of "folk music" as it came to be treated in the Anglosphere in the twentieth century. This is not to argue for or against said theories, but rather to register the way the chanty genre was adopted by an academic as an exemplar of theory.

Chanties become mixed up with ballads in the work of another literary figure: Britain's poet laureate, John Masefield (1878–1967). With seafaring being a distinct brick of Britain's self concept of national heritage, all of sailors' doings seem to have been brought into that crucible, and John "all I ask is a tall ship" Masefield took a special interest. For someone like Masefield, to separate chanties from ballads or one era of song from another was, perhaps, mere pedantry. All, in the English language, came under the banner of heritage. Similar to the view starting to be reflected in Whitmarsh's phrase "sea chanteys," for Masefield the category of "chanty" was a broad, perhaps even global one.

> They may be heard in ships of every nationality, but it is thought that they are most common in American, and rarest in French ships.[5]

Still the selections he made in repertoire, the lyrics he presented (many of which he surely composed), and the narratives he employed gave the genre a strong British emphasis. If I sound at all cynical in my description of Masefield's contribution to chanty discourse it is because the significance of such a distinctive understanding of chanties, presented by such a strong voice in the project of imagining English heritage, must be emphasized and Masefield's writing critiqued.

In a January 1906 article, Masefield presented thirteen chanties. With each appear, oddly enough, the corresponding musical scores for *piano accompaniment* that appeared in Davis and Tozer's most recent edition. This is strange indeed because the scores do not provide the *tunes* to the chanties! Perhaps it was an editorial oversight. And yet this is an important clue to Masefield's process. Davis and Tozer's versions of chanties were, up to this point, by far the most ballad-like and "literary." Being as far as possible from the doggerel found in other works, they were also arguably the most culturally "English" in their texts. For instance, whereas in the mouths of sailors on record, "Sally Brown" was a "bright mullata" and a "Creole lady" with a "nigger baby,"[6] Davis' Sally's "eyes are blue"[7] and Masefield (elsewhere) says, "Your cheeks are red, your hair is golden."[8] While sailors certainly may have imagined "Sally" however they wished, Davis and Masefield's choice to make her White (presumably) stands out, and this is just one example among other ways that they can be read as having an artificial-sounding "high society" cast. Masefield also says that he made use of L. A. Smith, the recent performance-ready eight-chanty collection by Bradford and Fagge (1904), and a few other less-notable articles.[9]

All this reliance of secondary-sources speaks to Masefield's *lack* of authority, despite his considerable clout in English literary discourse and his own teenaged sea experience training in the Merchant Marine, 1891–1895. While there is a certain amount of experienced-based originality in Masefield's work, much more is hearsay or fancy. For instance, he tells us that while he spent considerable time pumping during his sea service, "I have never heard a pumping chanty..." So, he is forced to say that,

> I am told that the usual pumping chanty is the halliard chanty of "Leave her, Johnny, leave her," one of the most excellent of all chanties...[10]

Clearly this work is not a field collection, nor does it represent the memories of a former chantyman; it is a type of popular folklore. By way of another example, Masefield claims that someone he knew made up the chanty "Come Roll Him Over."

> I knew a Danish sailor who passed his spare moments in inventing chanties. He had one half-finished specimen of which he was very proud. It may have been perfected since I knew him, and perhaps it is now well known "from Callao to Rio, by the west."[11]

Masefield then gives just one verse. Was this the "half-finished specimen"? If so, how is it that in one of his later publications the same chanty expanded to four verses?[12] Surely *that* one is not half-finished? One must suppose Masefield "finished" it, while presenting it as traditional. And then how do these verses (and more) turn up in the later collection of Stan Hugill, who had read Masefield, but who said he collected the song from a Barbadian man and ascribed it to rolling logs in the West Indies?[13] Masefield and Hugill are the only two editors to have the song in their collections. Something is fishy. Indeed, Masefield's leaps of fancy and laundering of Davis and Tozer's collection were, considered in hindsight, very bad for chanty discourse—if one cares about historical accuracy. Earlier editors may have tainted local waters, but this was like introducing a contaminate to the main water supply. This was concern for the English seafaring fantasy over fact. The same would often characterize the popular folklore stream of this era of discourse.

Masefield expanded his presentation of chanties in the anthology *A Sailor's Garland* (1906), a mix of verse related to the sea. The way in which Masefield frames the songs he presents is notable. Masefield was not alone among chanty writers in presenting conjecture as fact in the stories he told about the songs. One can discern his desire to connect chanties with much older English traditions and literature, and his characterization of individual items as such would prove attractive to later enthusiasts. So for example, Masefield implied that the chanty "A-Roving" (which he titled "The Maid of Amsterdam") was derived from Thomas Heywood's *The Tragedy of the Rape of Lucrece* (1608).[14] His "Lowlands Away," which shows evidence in its chorus of slavish copying from L. A. Smith, contains lyrics with a suspicious resemblance to an earlier ballad (included elsewhere in his collection), but which do not accord with other, field-collected versions—all suggesting that he manufactured it.[15] Masefield also states that "Haul on the Bowline" was "certainly in use in the reign of Henry VIII."[16] In general, the lyrics that he selected to present—and those he may have chose to omit—create a very English tone lacking the characteristics of American popular and African-American vernacular songs that had struck earlier writers. Lyrics and ideas from Masefield's attractive collection became amongst the most quoted or plagiarized in later chanty collections, and by their sheer ubiquity these contributed to how 20th-century audiences would envision the genre as a whole.

> *It seems exceedingly strange that among the great*
> *number of chanties lately noted there are none that we can*
> *confidently assign to a period as early as the 18th century.*
> —F. Kidson, 1908

The academic Folklore thrust of this era was led by the Folk-Song Society of England, in which a group of song collectors had gathered by the mid-1900s. The Society's *Journal* was the place to publish their collected songs, each of which might be commented upon briefly by various members of the circle. The circle's main interest was in songs of Britain and Ireland, among which chanties became lodged. Without wanting to overstate their position, I think it is fair to say that chanties were included because they were considered part of autochthonous British heritage, and that because they were included, in turn, they were more or less considered to be a subcategory of the category "English folk-song."

There are two implications of this. The first is that, because chanties and English folk-songs are grouped together as culturally English, chanties are assumed to spring from a common "English" sensibility. The type of melody (perhaps most important for these individuals), the lyrical themes, the type of language and singing style, and the manner of composition were generally presumed by default to emerge from the English heritage. Not to sell them short, these scholars certainly admitted differences when they were quite obvious, but, I would submit, such differences would tend to be read as variations and outside influences upon a common base, rather than evidence of other traditions' eminence. The second, related implication, then, was that the tendency was to view English heritage as the main trunk from which chanties were a branch, and characteristics atypical of the English core were exceptions rather than rules.

What is wonderful about the Society's collected chanties is that we have them for posterity and study. Unlike earlier authors of chanty collections, the academic folklorists recorded the musical and lyrical peculiarities of *specific* singers; they were relatively methodical and descriptive, as opposed to the "generic," quasi-composite versions of the chanties that had previously been the norm.

In the autumn of 1906, the *Journal of the Folk-Song Society* published its first batch of chanties, collected by Annie Gilchrist (1863–1954), with comments from Gilchrist, Frank Kidson, Lucy Broadwood, Cecil Sharp, and J. A. Fuller-Maitland.[17] There were three chanty texts and tunes gathered from Mr. W. Bolton of Southport, a 66 year-old retired sailor whose merchant service appears to have spanned the 1860s–80s. Davis and Tozer's collection and Whall's *Yachting Monthly* article were used as references. Gilchrist's commentary does not try to frame the items as English. Of "Shanandoah," she says that it is a "well known American chanty," and that "The tune appears to be of negro origin; it is at least of negro character."[18] The rendition of "Hogeye Man" is said to have "a decided negro flavour."[19] And "Across the Western Ocean," goes without comment, but it has the revealing lyric, "A dollar a day is a nigger's pay."[20]

The next batch of chanties appeared in the *Journal* in May 1908, collected by Percy Grainger and Harry Piggott.[21] These include four chanties sung by John Perring, an ex-sailor of Dartmouth (1908), and four sung by a Mr. Rosher, who seems to have collected them himself at an earlier time. Again Gilchrist is commenting, saying,

> "Storm Along," "Tom's gone to Hilo," and "Lowlands" are all chanties which strike me as negro in character, if not in origin.[22]

Gilchrist contributes an uncommon "negro chanty" ("Tapiocum"), "learnt on shipboard by a friend from the singing of an old coloured seaman."[23] The informant John Perring himself is explained to have called "Lowlands"

> …a "tipical" Negro chanty, sung by black sailors in the East Indian trade, in complaint at their being harder worked and lower-waged than white seamen.[24]

Thus at this point there is a strong voice for the African-American origin of chanties. If one accepts my characterization of the prior layer of discourse, one could say that some in the Society were still on that track. Yet others in the circle of folklorists, perhaps assuming the chanties should be English, are conflicted. Frank Kidson makes the following note about the age and geographic origins of chanties:

> When the history of the Sailor's Chanties comes to be written a great many difficult problems will have to be faced. For instance, it will have to be asked how it comes about that so many are, obviously, of American origin. Also, how it is that so many seem to centre round Mexico, or have place-names belonging to that quarter of the American Continent. Also, why we do not find any English, or other European coast or port included in the random rhymes which are strung together in chanties...It seems exceedingly strange that among, the great number of chanties lately noted there are none that we can confidently assign to a period as early as the 18th century.[25]

One might ask why this was necessarily an issue. If the evidence suggested that the chanties were American and were not older than the nineteenth century, why should one be looking to explain the contrary?

Publication by the Society continued with a 1914 issue containing chanties mostly collected by Sharp, with a couple contributions from Gilchrist.[26] The informants, between the ages of 58–84, presumably all learned their chanties in the second half of the nineteenth century: Charles Robbins (six, 1908–9), Wm. Wooley (one, 1908), Mrs. L. Hooper (one, 1904), Mr. Rapsey (two, 1906), W. Bolton (one, 1905), James Saunders (two, 1910), and John Allen (two, 1909). Their desk references are Alden, L. A. Smith, Whall (1910), Davis and Tozer, and Bradford and Fagge. The commentary says little about origins, though of "Reuben Ranzo" Gilchrist say that it "resembles an old morris-tune."[27]

Another batch came in 1916, collected by Sharp and Piggott.[28] These were collected from informants aged 61–78: Harry Perry (six, 1915), George Conway (two, 1914), Robert Ellison (one, 1914), H. C. Alison (one, 1914), and John Perring (seven, 1912). All collecting took place in England, except from Perry, an American ("a typical chanty-man of the old school"[29]) whom Sharp encountered on the American Liner *St. Paul*. The authors added Masefield and Bullen's collections to their references. For whatever reason—whether the method of collecting or the expectations of informants at this time in history—there were more ballad-type chanties ("Banks of Newfoundland," "Liverpool Girls") and English sailor-songs in this set. There is one "negro labour-song of the cotton stations of the Southern States" ("Southern Ladies," sung by Perry).[30] Much more comparison, however, is made here to British

Isles material. "Santiana" is said by Gilchrist to have "originally belonged to the old sea-ballad," "The Coasts of Barbary."[31] Gilchrist and Broadwood were keen on connecting "Haul on the Bowline" to earlier English or Irish sources. Gilchrist says, channeling Masefield, "This is probably one of our oldest English chanties," and Broadwood offers comparison tunes to support her idea that "This is apparently the opening phrase of a variant of the tune made famous by Tom Moore's arrangement... Moore took his air from Holden's *Irish Tunes...*"[32] We have reached, in the 1910s, the turning point that concluded my discussion of the previous layer, when the discourse was splitting off into an "English heritage" trajectory.

> *I have never even heard a chantey sung on board ship.*
>
> —C. Sharp, 1914

Cecil James Sharp (1859–1924), who had remained rather quiet throughout these articles, would seem to be the one to champion the English heritage perspective most. His work in the Appalachians, which sought to salvage an English repertoire supposed to be distinct in Britain, is a well-known example of his interests.[33] Similarly, Sharp's *English Folk-Chanteys* (1914), assembled from many of the chanties he had collected up to that point, reveals in its rather improbable title that his consideration of chanties was selectively old and English—or so he thought.

Culled from some 150 (including variants) from retired seamen around England that he claims to have documented, the collection contains a total of 60 chanties. The majority (46) came from John Short of Watchet, Somerset. Short (1839–1933), nicknamed "Yankee Jack" because of his service in an American ship,[34] started his deepwater career circa 1857–8 and retired circa 1873–5. Sharp tells us that he "throughout the greater part of his career was a recognised chanteyman."[35] Other informants, drawn from the Southwest of England and greater London, were Richard Perkins, Charles Robbins, George Conway, James Tucker, Henry Bailey, Mr. Rapsey, James Thomas, Captain Hole, and Robert Ellison. Unlike in the pages of the *Journal*, here the chanties are presented in rather idealized forms for performance. This means the selection of one tune, with piano accompaniment, and a sufficient stock of verses, which was achieved by compiling various renditions. So though Sharp's collection was based in field renditions, it was selectively compiled and contains a little editing, including bowdlerization.

Sharp's desk sources included Davis and Tozer, L. A. Smith, Bradford and Fagge, Bullen, and Whall. He remarks that the bibliography on chanties is "remarkably slender,"[36] but he does not appear to have attempted to do any historical research to discover other, less obvious sources. One can critique Sharp's relative ignorance of the subject. He had gained familiarity by this point, but what he did not know about chanties shows through now and again in misperceptions of what his informants sang. He admits as much:

> I have never even heard a chantey sung on board ship. But then I ap-
> proach the subject from its aesthetic side—my concern is solely with
> the music of the chantey and with its value as an art-product and this
> I contend is quite possible even for one who is as ignorant as I am of
> the technical details of the subject.[37]

In his intro to the collection, Sharp reveals his basic intent and biases. His *a priori* assumption is that this repertoire primarily belongs to a song tradition of the English people.

> The sailors' chantey is, I imagine, the last of the labour-songs to sur-
> vive in this country. In bygone days there must have been an enor-
> mous number of songs of this kind associated with every rhythmical
> form of manual labour...[38]

Why the English "must have" had songs for all kinds of labor, but none exist at present, is not stated. Yet on this basis, he seeks to connect the tunes to other English-language vernacular songs. This leads him to trace chanties back to the fifteenth century, following Whall's lead (and repeating his incorrect date):

> How old the chantey may be it is impossible to say, but that the cus-
> tom amongst sailors of singing in rhythm with their work was in
> vogue as far back at least as the fifteenth century, the vivid description
> of the voyage in "The Complaynt of Scotland" (c. 1450) places beyond
> question.[39]

In line with these assumptions, Sharp sought only to include songs with tunes of "folk-origin" and excluded popular song adaptations. He says that most of the tunes of chanties "must originally have been drawn from the stock of peasant-tunes with which the memory of every country-bred sailor would naturally be stored."[40]

Sharp talks about some items exhibiting "Negro influence," which seems to me a way of assuming again that some core English repertoire is at the center, which songs sung by Black people can only "influence"; Black song traditions cannot be at the center in this sort of discussion. Indeed, he calls "negro influence" on chanties a "vexed question."[41] Sharp uses musicological arguments, comparing what he believes to be the traits of Black American music, to argue against the significance of this influence. He goes on to say that, of course, with many Blacks having been in the sea service their culture has had some effect. Yet overall, "It is necessary, however, to distinguish between music of negroid origin and European music that has been modified by the negro."[42] As an example of this bias in his thinking, we see that he says the melody of "Haul Away Joe"—which we saw the 1858 Oberlin College author ascribed to Black rowers, and the sailor Jewell tied to an "old negro" minstrel song—is "singularly devoid of negro characteristics" and "one of our oldest chantey-tunes."[43] To his credit, however, Sharp concludes,

> However, I do not wish to be dogmatic. Sufficient material has not yet been amassed upon which to found a sound theory of the origin of the chantey-tune; and it may be that when further evidence is available the somewhat speculative opinions above expressed will need material modification.[44]

Sharp's academic voice and selective presentation, along with the voices of lay writers, created a path to envision an "English heritage" narrative for chanties. This would be all-important to their upcoming revival.

This layer was important to the historical record on chanties because it resulted in some of the last individuals to remember chanties having their repertoire documented fairly systematically. The academic collectors were objective in the sense that they were "outside of" their subject; they notated the lyrics and melodies that they heard, rather than collapsing personal memory of many years or creating "ideal" versions. Yet one of the very things that drove their work, an interest in English heritage, made some of the folklorists' discourse less than objective. Their methodology in what they chose to collect and where they would collect—England—shaped their results, and the way they then wrote about the material was riddled with assumptions. Nor were these assumptions tempered by historical research to understand what people of the past thought about chanties. Ideas jumped directly from medieval hauling chants to the present, in which British seaman who had sung chanties of late were considered to represent the tradition. And these ideas interacted with popular literary ideas to forge a new mold for subsequent writing and performances.

Key works

1906 Hutchison, "Sailors' Chanties," *Journal of American Folklore*

1906 Masefield, "Sea-Songs," *Temple Bar* (London)

1906 Masefield, *A Sailor's Garland* (London)

1906 Gilchrist, Kidson, Broadwood, Sharp, and Fuller-Maitland, "Sailors' Songs," *Journal of the Folk-Song Society* (London)

1908 Broadwood, Grainger, Sharp, Vaughan Williams, Kidson, Fuller-Maitland, and Gilchrist, "[Songs Collected by Percy Grainger]," *Journal of the Folk-Song Society*

1914 Sharp, Gilchrist, and Broadwood, "Sailors' Chanties," *Journal of the Folk-Song Society*

1914 Sharp, *English Folk-Chanteys* (London)

1916 Sharp, Gilchrist, Broadwood, Kidson, and Piggott, "Sailors' Chanties," *Journal of the Folk-Song Society*

Notes for chapter 4

1 On connections between the notions of "folk song" and "national music" in Anglophone discourse, see: David Harker, *Fakesong: The Manufacture of British "Folksong" 1700 to the Present Day* (Milton Keynes: Oxford University Press, 1985), 142–3, 170–1, 177.

2 Percy Adams Hutchison, "Sailors' Chanties," *Journal of American Folklore* 19.72 (1906): 17.

3 Ibid., 19.

4 Ibid., 23.

5 John Masefield, "Sea-Songs," *Temple Bar*, January 1906, 56.

6 E.g. even in the work of British bulldog, Whall, *Ships, Sea Songs*, third edition, 64.

7 Davis and Tozer, *Sailors' Songs*, third edition, 5.

8 John Masefield, ed., *A Sailor's Garland* (London: Macmillan, 1906), 316.

9 Masefield, "Sea-Songs," 80.

10 Ibid., 74.

11 Ibid., 67.

12 Masefield, *Sailor's Garland*, 314.

13 Stan Hugill, *Shanties from the Seven Seas: Shipboard Work-songs and Songs Used as Work-songs from the Great Days of Sail* (London: Routledge and Kegan Paul, 1961), 169.

14 Masefield, *Sailor's Garland*, 302.

15 Schreffler, "Twentieth-Century Editors," 40.

16 Masefield, *Sailor's Garland*, 303.

17 Annie G. Gilchrist, Frank Kidson, Lucy E. Broadwood, Cecil J. Sharp, and J. A. Fuller-Maitland, "Sailors' Songs, Collected by Annie G. Gilchrist," *Journal of the Folk-Song Society* 2.9 (1906): 236–49.

18 Ibid., 247.

19 Ibid., 249.

20 Ibid., 248. What I believe a lyric like this reveals is that the (original) creator of the lyric was a Black person. The lyric appears to express the grievance of being paid little or less than others, from a firsthand perspective.

21 Lucy E. Broadwood, Percy Grainger, Cecil J. Sharp, Ralph Vaughan Williams, Frank Kidson, J. A. Fuller-Maitland, and A. G. Gilchrist, "[Songs Collected by Percy Grainger]," *Journal of the Folk-Song Society* 3.12 (1908).

22 Ibid., 231.

23 Ibid., 236.

24 Ibid., 235.

25 Ibid., 238.

26 Cecil J. Sharp, A. G. Gilchrist, and Lucy E. Broadwood, "Sailors' Chanties," *Journal of the Folk-Song Society* 5.18 (1914).

27 Ibid., 38.

28 Cecil J. Sharp, A. G. Gilchrist, Lucy E. Broadwood, Frank Kidson, and Harry E. Piggott, "Sailors' Chanties," *Journal of the Folk-Song Society* 5.20 (1916).

29 Ibid., 298.

30 Ibid., 299.

31 Ibid., 298.

32 Ibid., 314.

33 Olive D. Campbell and Cecil J. Sharp, *English Folk Songs from the Southern Appalachians* (New York and London: G. P. Putnam's Sons), 1917.

34 Stan Hugill, *The Bosun's Locker* (Todmorden, Yorkshire: David Herron, 2006), 29.

35 Cecil J. Sharp, *English Folk-Chanteys* (London: Simpkin, Marshall, Hamilton, Kent and Co., 1914), xi.

36 Ibid., ix.

37 Ibid., x.

38 Ibid., ix.

39 Ibid., ix.

40 Ibid., xv.

41 Ibid., xv.

42 Ibid., xv.

43 Ibid., xvi.

44 Ibid., xvi.

V — RESOURCES FOR REVIVAL (1910s–1940s)

If the previous layer's main concern was to document the existing remains of a dead tradition, the next was driven by an interest in actually reviving it. By the 1920s, a full-fledged revival in chanty-singing was in effect. The logic of revival being an investment in heritage, the main concern was not for historical accuracy and weighing of evidence, but rather creating and solidifying supportive narratives.

> *A new war job under the sun has been created. It is*
> *Official Chantey Man for the American Merchant Marine.*
> —*New York Times*, Jan. 27, 1918

For sailors' chanties, any singing on land has tended to be related to what might be called "revival." This is because such singing is not of the working practice but rather of laypeople imagining the tradition through leisure-time performance. From this perspective, Davis and Tozer's performance-ready collection would seem to be first evidence of interest by "landsmen," though I have no direct evidence of it being *used* as such. There is, however, an incident on record that shows that at least one group of literary types had taken an interest already in the nineteenth century. In February 1895, at one of the weekly meetings of the Manchester Literary Club, one J. B. Shaw presented a paper on chanties.[1] It was accompanied by performances, with piano accompaniment. He certainly may have made up his own piano accompaniment, but it is quite possible, too, that the men who performed used the only published collection with piano parts at that point: Davis and Tozer. The news brief reporting the event quotes two sentences verbatim from Alden's 1882 article, which may also have been consulted for tunes, however it is Davis' spelling of "chanties" that is used. They also speak of "preserving" the songs, which, if it was expected performing would be apart of this preservation effort, would make this a prototype for the "folk-singing" approach. Were these the first rumblings of a revival?

Another deliberate, early effort to revive chanties, even if as a momentary novelty, resulted in the creation of a British eight-chanty collection by Bradford and Fagge, 1904. It is probably safe to assume that the role of Arthur Fagge (1864–1943), an English organist and choral conductor of note, was that of arranger. While the offerings of familiar chanties look original for the most part, there are numerous verses that are both contrived-sounding and too similar to Davis and Tozer's collection not to have been borrowed from it. As in that work, all the items are performance-ready with piano accompaniment. And as with effort to recreate chanty performances by the Manchester Literary Club, Bradford and Fagge's volume was met with enthusiasm for its potential use by laypeople. A review remarked, "All the songs… would be admirable for singing at smoking concerts and other festive gatherings. …an admirable addition to the library of choral societies."[2] *The Musical Times* for April 1906 notes that the Dulwich Philharmonic Society devoted the entire second half of a recent performance to these chanties, conducted by Fagge.[3]

Evidently this was just one part of a project, the other being an audio recording of all the arrangements. In early 1905 the Minster Singers of London, a house quartet of the Gramophone Company, performed on the same-titled *Old Sea Chanties*. This was released as four 10-inch phonograph discs on the Victor label, containing seven of the eight chanties (the short-haul chanty "Haul on the Bowlin'" was excluded).[4] These recordings were known to Masefield when he wrote in 1906, and, as mentioned earlier, the academic folklorists of that decade also consulted the collection of Bradford and Fagge. However, despite whatever impression it may have had at the time, it appears that later writers lost access to both the book and recordings.

Some sort of revival activity was certainly bubbling in the first decade of the twentieth century in Britain. Whall indicates the significant interest in the genre that shaped the publication—and re-publication—of his collection. For example, a concert of the Milford Choral Society, May 1913, included chanties on the program.[5] The scene was supported by retired sailors' and gentlemen's clubs who sang the chanties in a club setting as a form of camaraderie and, perhaps, affirmation of a connection to British identity. Bullen informs us, for instance, that he would hear "Sally Brown" and "Drunken Sailor" sung to lift the roof "on Saturday nights at London's Savage Club."[6] A bit later on, by the mid-1920s, the Seven Seas Club of London was singing chanties at the end of their monthly dinners.[7] One of the club members, John Sampson, was commissioned to compile a standardized collection of chanties by his fellows for this purpose. Sampson had experience with chanties during his sea service (1886–1898), but the items in his *The Seven Seas Shanty Book* (1927) show the heavy influence of prior publications' texts.

In America from the 1880s, social organizations unrelated to seafaring sometimes borrowed chanty items into their repertoire. A book of "students' songs" from the 1880s includes a parody version of "Rio Grande,"[8] and a turn of the century author noted, "Many familiar chanteys have been used in the more modern days as college songs."[9] "Rolling Down to Old Maui" (believed to be a chanty by some) and "South Australia" were introduced into the American Canoe Association's outings in 1885 and 1892, respectively.[10] Harvard University's *Book of Songs* for 1916 also included a version of "South Australia."[11]

A deliberate attempt to revive chanties amongst seamen occurred in the U.S. towards the end of the first World War. In early 1918, the American Merchant Marine appointed Stanton H. King (1867–1939) of Boston as its "Official Chantey Man." *The New York Times* called King "probably the best known chantey singer in the country."[12] Barbados-born King had sailed for a number of years in the merchant service (1880–86).[13] He was head of the Sailors' Haven mission at Charlestown, Massachusetts, and since 1893 had evidently been leading his colleagues in singing chanties there. By the summertime of 1918, singing chanties had become part of the daily recreational activities of merchant sailors on steam ships.[14] By November, it was claimed that chanty-singing was being "revived," and the prediction was made that soon to be produced phonograph records of chanties would spread their popularity far and wide.

> Chantey singing is being revived in the merchant marine, at least on the training ships which are preparing Young America, at the rate of 4,000 lads a month, for service on our vast new commerce fleets, and under the new order of things it will be possible for Bangor, Maine, and Mesa, Arizona to hear in the same hour the actual notes and phrases of such famous chanteys as "Shenandoah," "Bound for the Rio Grande" and "Blow the Man Down," for the record may have them hard and fast before spring flowers bloom again.[15]

During this time, King produced a standardized 24-chanty collection, *King's Book of Chanties* (1918).

> *...there must necessarily be some means of getting at the tune, unhampered by these individual idiosyncrasies...*
> —R. R. Terry, 1920

The individual whose work I believe most facilitated what might be called the "first" chanty revival, which peaked in the 1920s, was English musicologist and choir director Richard Runciman Terry (1865–1938). His maternal family came from a seafaring line. Terry's uncle, James Runciman (1852–1891, son of Coastguardsman Walter Runciman), had been a journalist and writer of sea stories that sometimes included somewhat unconvincing facsimiles of chanties.[16] Terry was an expert on liturgical music and player of the organ, but, due to inspiration from his family background, began a project of collecting chanties.

Terry entered the discussion in May 1915 with an address to members of the Royal Musical Association at London.[17] In his discourse, he often established his clout as an heir to a line of seafarers—though he could claim no direct experience himself—and distinguished himself from recent collectors like Cecil Sharp who had no such background. So although in the scheme of recent decades of discourse he had no particular authority over most writers, among his musical colleagues he spoke as an authority. Terry's first talk provided standard information about the genre, with an emphasis on issues of nomenclature. Somewhat original is his recognition, no doubt due to his musical acuity, of the influence of minstrel songs and other published material.

"Many a Christy Minstrel melody was adopted on board ship, for anything could be made into a Shanty"—or so he explains, in a later work, that a sailor once told him.[18] This does something to undermine Sharp's view of chanties being a rather more pure body of unwashed "folk" heritage. Terry calls for an "ideal collection" to be put together, a collaboration between sailor and musician.[19] The talk was accompanied by a performance of several items.

His audience responded enthusiastically to the "great chance of shanties being sung by men's choirs and so on…"[20] One observer noted that there was "a real hit of British style about it," and predicted that "in the coming years probably we shall cultivate more and more of the rollicking, true John Bull kind of song and tune."[21] This historical moment, when musical elites had come together in official performance and the performance was marked (i.e. after the developments of the previous layer) explicitly as British, might be seen as the real start of the first revival.

Terry went on to present his collected chanties, first in two articles in *Music and Letters*, 1920. In these he observes, as we have also seen, that writers had paid little attention while chanty-singing was "a living thing."[22] He blames this partly on the prudishness of the Victorian era and an alleged inability of individuals to overlook racy texts. He also blames it on the lack of access to sailors' songs by landsmen, and lack of ability to appreciate chanty tunes. While the former is not a situation that would have changed, the latter he supposes was overcome by the interest of folk-song collectors.[23] However, he does not acknowledge nationalistic motives that may have inspired those collectors.

Nevertheless, Terry is the first to really attempt a historiography, however brief. He critiques L. A. Smith's collection, noting that while the less rigorous style of her work, typical of her day, is understandable, it is still marred by incorrect versions of chanties and poor notation. Terry's critique is informed by the fact that, like Smith, he came from Newcastle and collected his chanties in Tyne seaports. Although Terry might not have realized that only a fraction of Smith's chanties was actually collected there, he rightly acknowledges that her collection had been often quoted as authoritative, and yet

> ...since the shanties in it were all collected in the district where I spent boyhood and youth, I am familiar with all of them, and can state definitely that they are in no sense authoritative.[24]

(If only Terry had known that most of the chanties in the Smith anthology were not collected by her in England!) Continuing, Terry says that Davis and Tozer's work can be ruled out as containing anything traditional. However, he has high praise for Whall's book, citing Whall's musical knowledge and declaring it to have that "necessary combination (which all the other collections lack) of seamanship and musicianship."[25] Terry establishes his own authority by saying that he grew up with chanties, "sung to me by sailor uncles and grand-uncles since I was a child."[26] He adds that he lived several years in the West Indies, "one of the few remaining spots where the shanty is still alive."[27] And he collected chanties, too, mostly from Northumbrian sailors. Still, in his commentary he reveals that, like Sharp, he lacked direct experience with chanties as they were performed aboard ship.[28]

Terry's method of presentation, as he explains, is to collate the lyrics and tunes he collected with the versions of songs he learned casually in his youth. These ideal versions would seem to be problematic, even contrary to his righteous critique of earlier collections, but he did not think so. He criticized the academic folklorists, too, for being *too* particular and descriptive.

> It is doubtless interesting to the folksonger to see in print shanties taken down from an individual sailor with his individual melodic twirls and twiddles. But since no two sailors ever sing the same shanty quite in the same manner, there must necessarily be some means of getting at the tune, unhampered by these individual idiosyncrasies, which are quite a different thing from what folk-song students recognise as "variants."[29]

He later reveals that there was some method to his work:

> As regards the tunes, I have adhered to the principle of giving each one as it was sung by some individual singer. This method has not been applied to the words. Consequently the verses of any given shan-

ty may have derived from any number of singers. Since there was no connection or relevancy between the different verses of a shanty, the only principle I have adhered to is that whatever verses are set down should have been sung to me at some time or other by some sailor or other.[30]

This, in fact, is not really different from what the academic folklorist Sharp did—when it came to his large collection.

Terry's work was soon organized into *The Shanty Book*, published in two parts, 1921 and 1926.[31] With its title alone, it was poised to become the source-book for folklore enthusiasts. In its forward, Sir Walter Runciman notably states that the tunes of chanties, "as folk-music, are a national asset."[32] In these publications Terry names his sources. These are: Sir Walter Runciman, Capt. John Runciman, James Runciman, W. J. Dowdy, Capt. R. W. Robertson, George Vickers, Richard Allen, F. B. Mayoss, Morley Roberts, and Sharp's star informant, John Short. We learn that he "camouflaged," i.e. bowdlerized, many of their verses that were considered "unprintable." There are sixty-five chanties in total.[33]

Between the publication of the first and second parts of *The Shanty Book*, Terry notes, there was a boom in chanties.[34] The collection's first part, in fact, had already become a main source for chanties during the 1920s revival. Why had the academic folklorists' works of the previous two decades not been equally utilized? Terry had his feet in the world of "legitimate" classical music performances; he was known in that world. Perhaps that is why his work was adopted over Sharp's. So it was Terry's book that became the basis for many early recordings. By 1928, commercial recordings of chanties, performed in the manner of classical concert singing, had been released on HMV, Vocalion, Parlophone, Edison, Aco, and Columbia labels.[35] Chanties like "Johnny Come Down to Hilo," in Terry's version, were more or less standardized through popular dissemination.

The present work has an intrinsic authenticity…
—Lincoln Colcord Jr., 1924

Terry's *The Shanty Book* marked the start of modern popular chanty collections, some with a more academic tone than others, but none with a truly scholarly approach. The first American entry to this body was *Roll and Go* (1924) by Joanna Colcord (1882–1960), a social worker by profession. Colcord's work would become one of the main sources for revival singers of the next era.

In the 1920s, she was largely engaging with the first part of Terry's collection (the second had not been published yet) along with the other major works that Terry had critiqued. Colcord, too, established her personal authority, however. Indeed, some may have thought that a woman was ill-suited as a chanty collector because the sailormen would be uncomfortable in opening up to her due to standing gender norms. The antidote to this potential doubting, much like in the case of Terry, was Colcord's family lineage and life experience. Her father was a ship's captain, Lincoln Alden Colcord, and Joanna was actually *born* on a sailing barque and raised on and around sailing vessels out of Searsport, Maine.[36] This was supposed to have put knowledge of chanties in her blood, as it were. Her brother, Lincoln Jr., writes in the introduction,

> The present work has an intrinsic authenticity; a compilation of folk songs, it was made by one who participated, both by life and inheritance, in the folk movement under discussion.[37]

And in her own words, Colcord says,

> The following examples of songs of the sea are drawn in part from my own memories of years spent on the blue water under sail from 1890 to 1899, mostly on voyages between New York and various ports on the China Sea. In part, they are songs learned from my father, who loved them and sang them well, and whose seagoing began about the year 1874.[38]

Yet Colcord did not so much write as if from her memories of growing up, but rather styled herself a song-collector. She thanks eight informants, including Harry Perry, the American who sang for Cecil Sharp. However, unlike Sharp she does not systematically tie her versions to specific informants. The result is that, with a casual reading, it looks like Colcord's collection is an assemblage of unique knowledge of the songs of "American sailormen." When one begins to crack the surface, however, one finds that most of the items are composites based in prior published sources. Colcord reprints several of the songs given by Robinson (1917); these instances are obvious if one knows his articles. For most other songs, if one compares the verses to earlier works, one will find that Colcord combined verses from them. Indeed, there is hardly an item in the collection that is original. It is true that Colcord's experiences may have *informed* how she shaped her presentation, and she did collect songs. Yet whatever unique information this may have revealed is, for the most part, hopelessly mixed in with derivative material. This makes Colcord's work of little use for historical study.

We are left then to consider Colcord's commentary, how she framed the chanties. Much is in the style of Whall, including brief speculations of the origins of each chanty, which are largely based on interpretive "reading" of certain words or phrases in the received texts. Earlier author's opinions are weighed or outright repeated, reinforcing narratives. Being an American, however, one of Colcord's ideas is of special note. This is her comment that previous collections had given the impression that chanty-singing was a British art.[39] Also notable is her comment on "...the American Negroes—the best singers that ever lifted a shanty aboard ship."[40]

Another woman who edited a popular chanty collection in this era also followed the method of compiling prior texts under the banner of experience with seafarers. A native of England, Cicely Fox Smith (1882–1954) lived in Victoria, Canada for some years, where she imbibed the stories of local sailors.[41] Primarily known as a fine poet of sea material, she published *A Book of Shanties* in 1927. It is less academic and more speculative than her contemporary Colcord's work, containing mostly composites, but also a few personal collections.[42] C. Fox Smith's commentary on origins is more haphazard and generally supports ideas of the British origin of the genre. Most sensationally, she dismissed Frank Bullen—whose work, one will recall, asserted an African-American origin of the chanty genre—by saying he "had nigger on the brain."[43]

C. Fox Smith was aware of the contemporary revival, even speaking of "shanty revivalists." It appears that the mainstream participants in lay chanty performance were so ignorant about their source material that Smith's own experience, in relation, carried a relative authority. She complained about the gut-less performances she was seeing, and was irked by the mispronunciation of the word "chanty," which inspired her to use the spelling "shanty."

> A few words...may not be amiss regarding the right way to revive the shanty. And in this connection, let me briefly describe a painful experience of my own as to how not to do it. It was at a music hall which shall be nameless. The curtain rose, revealing one of those impossible stage inns...called "The Jolly Tar," or something equally improbable. Outside this preposterous establishment were seated at a small table three large mariners, whose costume—an artistic blend of jerseys, sea-boots, cheesecutter and stocking caps—suggested that they had made an indiscriminate raid on the slop chest at the Sailor's Home. Quoth one of these worthies to another: "Let's have a tchahntey!" and amid encouraging cries of "A tchahntey—yes, a tchahntey!" the individual addressed rose, and with a wealth of dramatic gesture, laying aside his

churchwarden pipe, sang—well, I just forget what he did sing! It was too painful to listen to![44]

These authors in this layer may have known more than average about the topic, but it would be a mistake to assume that they knew chanties as they were historically. Theirs was a new establishment of authority, a sort of amateur folklorist's authority, about the nature of the genre. And their less knowledgeable readers had little choice but to accept their authority. The driving principle seems to have been that anyone who had contemporary knowledge of *seafaring life* would naturally have more knowledge about chanties.

With this paradigm set, a number of similar collections appeared in the 1920s through 1940s. Catering to the contemporary interest, each author would bring some personal experience of chanties, generally from the time after they had died out, and fill out their collection mainly with material drawn from and couched within narratives and classification schemes of earlier writers. Of these I will cite just one other representative example, Frank Shay, who edited *American Sea Songs and Chanteys* (1948). Shay (ca. 1889–1954), who grew up in New York, was a sailor before World War I. He says he heard his first chanty while serving aboard a tanker in 1915, when the ship's power was burnt out and some work consequently had to be done by hand.[45] As his experience was of the memory of chanties, revived as it were, his impressions of the genre were mostly based in writing. Similarly to Whitmarsh (1903), he concluded that, "The chantey, though English in origin, early became American in content."[46]

Judging from the number of publications and recordings, the height of this first chanty revival occurred around 1927. Davis and Tozer's collection was re-released in that year. These works changed the face of what the public viewed to be "sea shanties," including a sharp rise in that term and the generalization of it to popularly include all number of sailor songs. Folklorists such as Broadwood and Fox-Strangways could now construct such concepts as "Greek chanty-singing in the early centuries of the Christian era,"[47] which would have been nonsensical to 19th-century chantymen.

In sum, the derivative or unsystematic popular works of this layer, whose artificial correlations seem to corroborate one another, served to standardize the repertoire of chanties and reset widely-held ideas about them. The false correlations and emphasis on certain narratives formed a dense layer of conventional wisdom that reinforced the concept of British and/or White origins. Indeed, even with statements noting the individual contributions or excellence of Black chanty-singers, the re-envisioned narrative of many chanty items cohered to form a sort of "evidence" that the root of the tradition lay elsewhere. The more careful work of R. R. Terry is chiefly significant, not for its scholarship, but for providing a solid base of usable musical material. The works of this layer would become the go-to works for later generations of revivalists.

Key works

1904 Bradford and Fagge, *Old Sea Chanties* (London)

1915 "Sea Songs and Shanties." *Proceedings of the Royal Music Association* (London)

1918 King, *King's Book of Chanties* (Boston)

1920 Terry, "Sailor Shanties," *Music and Letters* (Oxford)

1921 Terry, *The Shanty Book: Part I* (London)

1924 Colcord, *Roll and Go: Songs of American Sailormen* (Indianapolis) [Enlarged as *Songs of American Sailormen*, 1938]

1926 Terry, *The Shanty Book: Part II* (London)

1927 C. F. Smith, *A Book of Shanties* (London)

1927 Sampson, *The Seven Seas Shanty Book* (London)

1928 Broadwood and Fox-Strangways, "Early Chanty-Singing and Ship-Music," *Journal of the Folk-Song Society* (London)

1931 Bone, *Capstan Bars* (Edinburgh)

1948 Shay, *American Sea Songs and Chanteys* (New York)

Notes for chapter 5

1 Manchester Literary Club, *Papers of the Manchester Literary Club*, Vol. 21. (Manchester: John Heywood, 1895), 432–3.

2 "Reviews and Notices of Books," *The Lancet*, May 5, 1906, 1253.

3 "Suburban Concerts," *The Musical Times*, April 1, 1906, 262.

4 See: http://victor.library.ucsb.edu/index.php/talent/detail/6859/Minster_Singers_Vocal_group. An advertisement in *The Smart Set* magazine, November 1905, lists the Minster Singers' recordings:

> 61145 "The Capstan Bar";
>
> 61146 "Blow, My Bully Boys" and "Sally Brown";
>
> 61147 "Whisky Johnny" and "Shenandoah";
>
> 61148 "Rio Grande" and "Blow the Man Down."

5 "Country and Colonial News," *The Musical Times*, May 1, 1913, 337.

6 Bullen and Arnold, *Songs of Sea Labour*, xiii.

7 "Sea Chanteys Kept Alive. Sailors' Club in London is Collecting and Preserving the Old Songs of Sail," *New York Times*, November 7, 1926, SM18.

8 W. H. Hills, ed., *Students' Songs*, thirteenth edition (Boston: Rand Avery, 1887), 34.

9 Lahee, "Sailors' Chanteys" 18.

10 "Canoeing," *Forest and Stream* 39.9 (1892): 188. Intriguingly, William Alden, author of the important 1882 article in *Harper's*, was a founding member of the American Canoe Association. [http://www.americancanoe.org/?page=History]

11 Associated Harvard Clubs, *Book of Songs* (Chicago: Lakeside Press, 1916), 22.

12 "Official Chantey Singer," *New York Times*, January 27, 1918.

13 *Heirlooms Reunited* blog [http://heirloomsreunited.blogspot.com/2010/04/stanton-h-king-born-1867barbados.html] contains information on King's biography from *The Fort Wayne News And Sentinel* (14 Feb 1918) and *Nashua Reporter* (7 Mar 1918).

14 Henry Howard, "Manning the New Merchant Marine," *Pacific Marine Review* 15 (1918): 105; James H. Collins, "Vikings of the Future," *St. Nicholas* 45.10 (1918): 883.

15 "Carrying the Sea Atmosphere Inland," *Shipping*, November 16, 1918, 13.

16 See e.g.: James Runciman, *Skippers and Shellbacks* (London: Chatto and Windus, 1885), 81, 142.

17 Richard Runciman Terry, "Sea Songs and Shanties," *Proceedings of the Royal Music Association* 11.41 (1915).

18 Richard Runciman Terry, "Sailor Shanties (I)," *Music and Letters* 1.1 (1920): 43.

19 Ibid., 137.

20 Ibid., 139.

21 Ibid., 139.

22 Terry, "Sailor Shanties (I)," 35.

23 Ibid., 35.

24 Ibid., 37.

25 Ibid., 37.

26 Ibid., 37.

27 Ibid., 37.

28 For example, Terry speculates as to how chantymen conducted and positioned themselves while they were leading chanties. Richard Runciman Terry, "Sailor Shanties (II)," *Music and Letters* 1.3 (1920): 259.

29 Terry, "Sailor Shanties (II)," 264.

30 Richard Runciman Terry, *The Shanty Book: Part I* (London: J. Curwen and Sons, 1921), xii.

31 The two parts were brought together and reprinted in 2009 under the title, *The Way of the Ship*.

32 Terry, *The Shanty Book: Part I*, iii.

33 Ibid., xii.

34 Richard Runciman Terry, *The Shanty Book: Part II* (London: J. Curwen and Sons, 1926), vii.

35 Llewelyn C. Lloyd, "Folk-songs of the Sea: Shanties on the Gramophone," *Gramophone*, March 1927.

36 For a documentation of Colcord's remarkable childhood, see: Parker Bishop Albee, *Letters from Sea, 1882–1901: Joanna and Lincoln Colcord's Seafaring Childhood* (Gardiner, ME: Tilbury House; Penobscot Marine Museum, 1999).

37 Joanna C. Colcord, *Songs of American Sailormen* (New York: Norton, 1938), 20. It seems that Lincoln Colcord Jr. was not only vouching for Joanna's nautical experience, but also preemptively making the case for a *woman's* ability to write on the subject.

38 Colcord, *Songs of American Sailormen*, 35.

39 Ibid., 31–2.

40 Ibid., 32.

41 Charles Ipcar, ed., *Sea Songs of Cicely Fox Smith* (Richmond, ME: Charles Ipcar, 2010), iv. Ipcar states that Smith lived there from 1905–1913. In a later Internet posting after further research, however, he adjusted these dates to 1911–1913. <http://mudcat.org/thread.cfm?threadid=9242&messages=110#3802030>

42 The fragment, "Bound to California" is an example. Cicely Fox Smith, *A Book of Shanties* (London: Methuen, 1927), 27–9.

43 Smith, *Book of Shanties*, 10.

44 Ibid., 14–5.

45 Frank Shay, *American Sea Songs and Chanteys* (New York: Norton, 1948), 15.

46 Ibid., 12.

47 Lucy E. Broadwood, and A. H. Fox-Strangways, "Early Chanty-Singing and Ship-Music," *Journal of the Folk-Song Society* 8.32 (1928): 58.

VI — DEVELOPMENTS IN FOLKLORE STUDIES (1920s–1960s)

Interest in chanties in the 1920s–40s inspired more research in academic folklore, which had continued to evolve in its methods and style. As opposed to the sort of "secondary source collating" that was happening, what we might call real "collecting" was still going on, of a reasonably objective, descriptive nature, though it had little influence on the revival. This work was being done by American and Canadian researchers who, not surprisingly and in contrast to the 1900s–1910s scholars, had less interest in hunting for lost British heritage. However, they were not uninterested in documenting their own nations' heritage.

> *...the shanties which are to–day remembered with pleasure are almost exclusively of white origin, and constitute a not unimportant branch of folk–song.*
> —L. G. Carr Laughton, 1923

We begin this section by noting the work of someone who does not quite fit the trend being identified in this chapter—though nor does he fit the trends in the preceding chapters. This anomaly provides me an excuse to briefly review the participants in these trends. In the first layer we heard from Contemporary Observers, people who were ear-witnesses to chanty-singing in ships during its global heyday, 1850s–70s. Commentators saw chanty-singing in vessels as something connected with America, and presented it more practically than romantically. Understanding the genre to be no older than their current century, these writers also had no anxiety when pointing out similarities to singing associated particularly with Black people. The sharp decline of chanty-singing in ships in the 1880s brought about the Early Collectors, who memorialized chanties—by then a known quantity—within edited collections. The romanticization of chanties, concurrent with the disappearance of their use in ships, created an interesting environment of salvage and revision in the early part of the twentieth century. One group of discussants (chapter 3) were past eyewitnesses, Remembering Observers, who sought to recollect what they had heard. Their accounts present a mixed picture of anecdotal evidence filtered through competing current narratives in a time when a nationalistic, anti-modernity view from Folklore was ascending. Accompanying them were the Early Folklorists. They were largely British, inexperienced with chanty-singing practice, and interested in what the chanty genre could offer to the project of Anglocentric Folklore. They documented the recollections of their contemporaries, the Remembering Observers, putting their texts and remarks in "proper" academic frame. The product of this critical mass of discourse was a drawing-room revival of "sea shanties," in turn creating a market for popular resources—texts with a full compliment of appealing verses, generic melodies without "twirls and twiddles," and a simple accompanying narrative without the admission, "I don't know." Indeed, the Popular Editors made sure to instill confidence in their readers by connecting themselves to seafaring in some fashion. It is at this point that we see the next layer of contribution, from the Middle Folklorists, the next generation of academic discussants. This group, largely American and, by extension, unable to follow the picture of an ethnic nation contiguous with an old political nation, were forced to raise questions about chanty history that the Early Folklorists neatly skirted. They raised these questions and yet, we must note, they were not historians. Their academic rigor came in the form of favoring larger samples over anecdotal evidence and of being strictly descriptive.

The above referenced work in its own category, which nonetheless connects discursive threads, is a single article by British naval historian Leonard G. Carr Laughton (1871–1955). Carr Laughton, son of a naval historian himself, was a founder of the Society for Nautical Research; his article was published in the maritime scholars' organ *The Mariner's Mirror* in 1923. Like the Early Folklorists, he was a British academic, and it seems he did subscribe to contemporary views about folk-song and autochthonous English heritage. His remarks are meant for an academic audience, and the significance of this work lies in its influence on the discourse of future scholars, not laypeople. Somewhat like the Popular Editors, his connection to things maritime would seem important; he could claim superior authority in a discussion where mariners are supposed to be the focus. Carr Laughton, however, neither collected chanties nor documented their texts and musical forms, and thus he relied upon both the Early Folklorists and Popular Editors. In contrast, he sought to ask questions that one must answer through the study of history. It was the Remembering Observer Whall who first made attempts of this type, presenting his more or less authentic yet anecdotal recollections alongside claims about Elizabethan chanty origins and the inferiority of African-American contributions to the canon. Carr Laughton's work follows Whall, without the privilege of eye-witness observation yet with better academic rigor toward the historical details. With so little of historical substance in previous works, Carr Laughton's was important for providing the Middle Folklorists with ideas. It might be considered the first article to attempt a history of chanty-singing and this, in fact, was his stated reason for writing it.[1]

Carr Laughton makes a number of ambitious claims that address rather than avoid (e.g. in the manner of the Early Folklorists) the issues of chanties' national and cultural origins or influences. Stating his opinion that the work-songs included in Dana's mid-1830s account do not appear to be of African-American origin, and that these same songs seem to disappear after 1860, Carr Laughton seeks to explain what conditions operated upon shipboard life such that the repertoire of chanty-singers came to include so many African-American songs. So it is a change in the world of "shantying" that he is addressing, which sets him apart from the Early Folklorists and their relatively static view of history. His suggestion of a formative African-American influence was, however, not new. As early as Alden it was claimed that chanties were connected to Black cotton-stowers in the American South, and this idea had become common enough even to appear in *The History of American Music* (1908), but English discourse outside America had regressed so far[2] that what he goes on to say about African-American influence was "hitherto unnoticed."[3]

Carr Laughton begins the explanation with a bland acknowledgement that English seamen were familiar with Black singers "from an early date" because Black seamen existed among the crews of English ships, and that this would have prepared the ground for later intercultural borrowing.[4] He goes on to describe the cotton trade as the framing factor of chanty development.

> The known facts support the view that negro shanties, and the term shanty were introduced during the rise of the cotton trade, and it seems likely that it was in the forties that the negro shanties began to oust the old working songs.[5]

Carr Laughton textures his narrative by recognizing different periods of development. Currently available evidence more or less supports his characterization of these periods.

> ...it would appear that few, if any, shanties have been introduced since about 1860. The great constructive period seems to have been from 1830 to 1860; from 1860 to 1880 the greatest possible use was made of the songs already established; from 1880 onwards songs were adapted to altered conditions, but nothing new was permitted.[6]

Decades later, Stan Hugill paraphrased these ideas, with no obvious credit given to Carr Laughton, in the historical overview that begins his first book.[7]

However, much of Carr Laughton's work takes the reader through Whall's *Complaynt of Scotland*-based narrative, only with more rigor and citation. Though he finally concludes that, "shantying, in the form in which we know it, hardly existed before the 19th century,"[8] and though he wrote earlier that the term "shanty" was introduced during the rise of the cotton trade (i.e. under the influence of contact with African-American culture), he nonetheless attempts to connect the dots of all vocalization in Anglophone ships to suggest the appearance of a continuous phenomenon of "shantying." The wording here is important. "Shantying" can mean "chanty-singing," in other words, "to sing in the chanty genre." Compare a word one might invent, "violining," which would mean "violin-playing" or "to play on the violin." However, in Carr Laughton's case, of "shantying" we are meant to understand "to sing while at work (at sea)." Rather than the specificity of "violining," we would have something like "fiddling," which could include such distant events as a performance of Brahms' *Concerto in D Major* and what Emperor Nero is accused of having done while Rome burned! With this principle in place, the evidence-based nature of the study comes to clash with a biased desire for a particular outcome, in the article's very last paragraph. Invoking "folk-song," he regresses to a position of British Early Folklorists in treating "shantying" as a "White" activity upon which African-American practice had only a fleeting influence.

> Whatever the case may have been latterly, there is no doubt that some sixty years ago seamen took a proper pride in their shantying. The resistance offered at that period to the rising tide of negro melody is evidence of this. The negro songs indeed prevailed for a time; but the shanties which are to-day remembered with pleasure are almost exclusively of white origin, and constitute a not unimportant branch of folk-song.[9]

There is no explanation as to why he stated that during the 1860s (i.e. when "the greatest possible use was made of the songs already established") there was, simultaneously, a resistance to "negro melody." Nor can we verify the chanty items "remembered with pleasure." What may be said is that future historical studies of chanties would require investigation of sources outside the narrow corridor of English shipboard life.

The negro on the docks heard them sung by white sailors.
—R. W. Gordon, 1927

Robert Winslow Gordon (1888–1961), originally of Bangor, Maine, studied English at Harvard (1906–16) under the ballad scholar George Lyman Kittredge. In 1917–24 while working as assistant professor in UC Berkeley's Department of English, Gordon collected over a thousand songs, including chanties, sung to him by retired seamen in the ports of San Francisco and Oakland, California. Hundreds were recorded on wax cylinders.[10] Gordon "hoped to learn from this large body of data something of the role that Afro-American traditions and popular minstrel show materials played in the development of the sea shanty."[11] In 1925, Gordon moved from Berkeley to the family home of his wife in Darien, Georgia. There he began a project to record Black songs of the area, including rowing songs that had died out elsewhere.[12] This would give him a unique perspective on the place of chanties within the wider American song traditions.

In 1928, Gordon was appointed the first director of the nascent Archive of American Folk Song at the Library of Congress.[13] There he continued to gather manuscripts of chanties submitted to him. Gordon published two relevant articles in *The New York Times*, January 1927, and later released the book *Folk-songs of America* (1938). He never released any published collection specific to chanties, however, so access to his work was effectively limited for those not visiting the archive.[14]

In his published writing Gordon concluded that the African-American songs of Georgia were "related to chanteys" and called them, in fact, "work chanteys."[15] However, he believed that the African-Americans' work-songs that corresponded to known sailor-chanties were borrowed from White sailors.

> The negro on the docks heard them sung by white sailors. He borrowed them with minor variations. Those he liked he rebuilt to suit better his own tasks and later he invented new chanties on the old model.[16]

As fortune would have it, another individual ended up collecting folklore of the Gullah culture of Georgia in the community of St. Simon's, not far away from Gordon's activities. Lydia Parrish moved from her native New Jersey to the area in 1909, whereupon she heard the uncommonly preserved singing of former slaves. She went on to record songs in the 1930s, and her book *Slave Songs of the Georgia Sea Islands* (1942) contains chanties sung by the local men, several of which are unique variants of well-known deepwater items. Parrish's informants Joe Armstrong and Henry Merchant had once led stevedore crews, loading lumber and stowing cotton. Indeed, the memory of chanties was still alive in everyday life.

> In Brunswick, vessels are still loaded to the musical chant of "Sandy Anna"; freight cars at the sugar terminal are shunted for short distances to the rhythm of "Old Tar River," and the cabin in front of my house was moved on rollers from Kelvin Grove to the significant tune of "Pay Me My Money Down!"[17]

Parrish's is an important latter-day study of a region where some of the earliest African-American work-songs flourished.

> *Chanteymen were naturally quick to press into service*
> *aboard ship the Negro gang-work songs...*
> —J. M. Carpenter, 1938

The next major collector of chanties was James Madison Carpenter (1888–1984), who received a Ph.D. from Harvard. As a student of English Department Professor George Lyman Kittredge (like Robert Gordon), he was encourage to collect material that could be used as field evidence of English-language vernacular traditions, in the vein of ballad scholar Francis James Child.[18] However, as biographers Jabbour and Bishop opine, Carpenter perhaps did not fit the mold of other folk-song scholars of the age. He never presented the findings of his expansive, comparative fieldwork in any high-profile publications, and he never became established in a major university position though he continued to make field collections.[19] Carpenter's enormous repository of manuscripts and recordings was acquired by the Library of Congress in 1972. As with Gordon's collection, Carpenter's remained more or less unstudied until the later part of the twentieth century. Of note, Roy Palmer included some of the chanties in *The Oxford Book of Sea Songs* (1986), and Bob Walser (of more below) started working with the collection in the 1990s.[20]

Carpenter's represents the largest field collections of chanties. In 1927, he made collections from sailors in Massachusetts and at Sailors' Snug Harbor (Staten Island). In the summer of 1928 and for a full year in 1929, he continued the work in Britain and Ireland.[21] The results went into his dissertation, "Forecastle Songs and Chanties" (1929). Among the collection were some nine-ty-eight different chanties[22] out of a total of about 375 original recordings,[23] many of which he made using a portable Dictaphone machine.

In all, Carpenter collected chanties from some sixty-one men. Most of Carpenter's remarkable array of informants first went to sea in the 1870s and '80s, but included two who first went to sea before 1850. Edward Robinson of Sunderland, among the oldest men interviewed, first went to sea in 1846, shipping to America, Canada, and the West Indies. The chanties sung by Robinson seem to match his era well. He knew the early (and later less common) song "Cheer'ly Man," and chanties that otherwise can be tied to the 1840s (2), 1850s (10), and 1860s (2), along with one I cannot otherwise tie to earlier than the 1870s. Mark Page, also of Sunderland, first shipped in 1849 and left the trade in 1879. Page's repertoire included chanties from the 1840s (2), 1850s (4), 1860s (5), and three others that are hard to determine. James Forman of Leith, another old-timer, first shipped in 1856. The singers James Wright (Leith, shipped 1864), Robert Yeoman (Dundee, shipped 1869), Andrew Salters (Greenock, shipped 1872), Richard Warner (Cardiff, shipped 1877), William Fender (South Wales, shipped 1878), Rees Baldwyn (South Wales, shipped 1879), John Conway (Wiclow, Ireland, shipped 1882), and Alexander Blue (Greenock, shipping dates unknown), all indicated that they had learned certain chanties from experiences observing cotton-, sugar-screwing, and other stevedores in the West Indies and the African-American South. Fender's singing is especially notable for what might be considered distinctive "Black" vocal style characteristics.

Much like with Sharp and his cohort, as with Terry, the collected material mostly or entirely comes from White British or American informants, putting it within a particular stylistic range.[24] However, while Gordon, by contrast, recorded both White and Black singers of work-songs and concluded the latter were influenced by the former, Carpenter felt the opposite. Carpenter wrote four articles on chanties for *The New York Times*, in July 1931 and October 1938, in which he stated that African-American work-songs were a major contributing element to the form of chanties.

> These working choruses, frequently taken from the Negro laborers of different countries, especially the Southern States, existed in large numbers, for the Negro required a song to lighten his work. I have found scores that have never been published. Most of them are of the simplest nature, being little more than a rhythmical, melodious drone of nonsense syllables. But created in the midst of toil and chanted over and over again for the brief respite that they gave from its weary monotony, they bear a hidden charm that the sailor was quick to dis-

cover. In the more pensive ones he must have found something of the strange satisfaction and restfulness of the chant.[25]

And elsewhere:

> Indeed, it is not surprising to find a fairly large proportion of the chanteys coming from the American South. Chanteymen were naturally quick to press into service aboard ship the Negro gang-work songs—with their droll fun, languorous cadences, and well-worn rhythm.[26]

Further, he reasons from analysis of his data that chanties did not exist in great numbers until after Dana's time[27]—ideas that square with the historical evidence now available.

Remarkably, Carpenter arrived at those ideas without much of a literary survey; his dissertation indicates that his book sources were just the 19th-century ones of Alden, Luce, and L. A. Smith. His evidence was the recordings he gathered and the statements of his informants. The troupe of folklorists in Sharp's school also did fieldwork, but their style differed in that they always accompanied their discussions with a summary of what prior authors on the subject had said. I think that all that secondary-source reading, though undoubtedly important in scholarship, colored their presentations in a way that Carpenter's, perhaps, was not. Indeed, so far as they were mostly White British sailors in the first half of the twentieth century, Carpenter and Sharp's informants were not very different demographically. One must find something different in the methodology of Carpenter that would lead to such a different opinion. I would offer that the difference was that the British folklorists had eventually come to be looking for something exclusively (or preferably) "folk" and British. If Carpenter was looking for something American, he made an odd choice in focusing on Britain; his conclusions came even in spite of his methodological choices.

> *And show us where the pull…*
> *where the pushing comes…*
> —A. Lomax, 1939, interviewing Dick Maitland

Perhaps the ultimate American comparativist and most indefatigable fieldworker was Alan Lomax, so it is not surprising that chanties and related work-songs came into his net. Like Gordon and Carpenter, Lomax had been a student of Prof. Kittredge at Harvard. He never presented himself specifically as a chanty collector, however. When Lomax presented chanties it was often with reference and deference to other collectors. In this light, it is not really Lomax's statements on chanties that are of interest, but rather the recordings he made—often without realizing, it seems, that the material was part of the chanty repertoire. Lomax's chanty material is spread around many collections and still waiting to be gathered together under this theme. And while Revival singers have retrospectively made the connection and brought some of Lomax's material into their repertoire, there is still much chanty material that, either through opaque cataloging or its difference from familiar versions, goes unrecognized.

The first batch of Lomax's relevant material was collected while he was in the Bahamas in 1935. This was done amongst crews of spongers who worked from sailboats. They sang in a unique multi-part style that was not necessarily anything like chanties elsewhere. Nevertheless certain songs were related to more familiar items of chanty repertoire.[28]

Lomax next followed in the footsteps of Lydia Parrish, visiting St. Simons first in 1935 with Zora Neale Hurston, then returning in 1959 and 1960 to record. What he documented included performances by the "original" singers, who had been organized already in Parrish's day into a revival group of sorts, the Spiritual Singers of Georgia.[29]

Around the same time (1960), Lomax recorded another of the African-American maritime work-song traditions, in Virginia. Net fishermen for the small commercial fish called menhaden had a tradition that they also called "chanteys," and men from this dying profession had organized themselves into a group called the Bright Light Quartet. The form of these songs was a bit different from the sailor-chanties, and repertoire did not correspond, but it is notable that the men explicitly considered them to be chanties.

Perhaps the most notable body of songs collected by Lomax, in relation to familiar chanties, came from a fieldtrip to the Caribbean in 1962. These included correspondences in Anguilla, Grenada, Nevis, and Trinidad and Tobago. Not only the work-songs, but the game-songs also show correspondences that, due to their classification and unfamiliar accents (i.e. from American and British perspective), could be overlooked (and have been) by scholars.

In comparison to these African-American and Caribbean items, Lomax's own collection of deepwater songs from White sailors is slight. One batch was from Albert H. Rasmussen (1883–1972), a retired Norwegian sailor whom Lomax recorded with Peter Kennedy in London, 1955. Rasmussen was a writer and historian, and while his presentation of chanties was not unconscious, his renditions provide some unique variants and interesting insight on how he used to sing chanties. These recordings are significant as comparatively clear audio examples of the singing of an authentic chantyman in a slow, measured style. Another batch of Lomax's collection comes from 19th-century deepwater sailors Richard Maitland and John M. "Sailor Dad" Hunt. Maitland gave Lomax thirty-seven items (chanties and sea songs) in 1939, and Hunt gave eleven in 1935 and 1941, all of which are in the Library of Congress. When Lomax famously asked Maitland to tell him where the "pulls" were in the capstan chanty "Paddy, Lay Back,"[30] it revealed his rather cursory understanding of chanties. Lomax found himself an incidental collector of chanties that still await cataloguing.

> *…the practice of shantying, while it can hardly have*
> *been silenced completely during this period [17th–18th*
> *centuries], must have suffered a sharp decline.*
> —W. M. Doerflinger, 1951

William Main Doerflinger (1910–2000) gathered deepwater chanties from retired sailors in Nova Scotia and at Sailors' Snug Harbor, Staten Island, in the 1930s and early 1940s. Doerflinger's work differs from that of other collectors of his type in that it was realized in a book that was both extensive and accessible. *Shantymen and Shantyboys: Songs of the Sailor and Lumberman* (1951) contains a set of over 65 original, unmixed chanty renditions collected by Doerflinger, descriptively presented (transcriptions were made by music experts). Doerflinger did omit some verses considered unsuitable for printing, but he did not bowdlerize anything. Textual and melodic variations are described rather meticulously. The book contains more extensive historical background and cross-referencing than had even been done. This makes it one of the most rigorous presentations of deepwater chanties available. The book's only downsides are the comparatively small number of chanty items it contains (the book also includes sailors' and lumbermen's leisure songs) and Doerflinger's tendency to introduce chanties within well-worn narratives, some of which are contradicted by the evidence now available.

Doerflinger's chapter on "The Rise of Shantying" was the most complete statement to date on the development of the genre. Among Doerflinger's ideas was that the emergence of chanties in literature around the 1830s represented a *rejuvenation* of chanty-singing after the War of 1812. He retains the medieval English origins narrative (cf. Whall, Carr Laughton) while emphasizing the factor of practical shipboard needs to explain trends of the genre's vitality.[31]

The idea is that the need for chanty-singing waned in 18th century vessels, which were over-manned for war or protection from pirates. Where shipboard work-songs began to receive mention in the nineteenth century, Doerflinger interprets this as a revival of the ancient art of chanty-singing. The reason for this revival was a new or re-emerged need for work-songs in small crew, hard-driving Yankee merchant ships.[32] Doerflinger also emphasizes that White sailors were engaged in cotton-stowing, and only softly implies (but does not explicitly state) that they learned African-American song material in that context.[33]

This layer of discourse, on more developed folklore studies, can be distinguished from the prior layer of popular collections in that the folklore scholars tie their songs to specific individuals and give some information about who those people were. In this way, we can contextualize their findings somewhat. Doerflinger's major informants include, first, Richard (Dick) Maitland (born 1857) of New York, who first went to sea ca. 1869–70. Also recorded by Alan Lomax, Maitland shipped in Yankee vessels at a time when shipboard chanty-singing was at its peak. Captain Patrick Tayluer, born in Eastport, Maine, first went to sea in 1885. He sailed in American and British vessels. Tayluer seems to have been a great improviser, and some of his renditions are quite extensive in their number of verses. His recordings, made in 1942 and 1948, are in the Archive of Folk Song, Library of Congress. James P. Barker, born in Cheshire, England was one of the later ones to go to sea, in 1889. He rounded Cape Horn 41 times and was captain of America's last commercial ship, *Tusitala* of New York. Barker's chanties included two notable items ("Rise Me Up from Down Below" and "Hello, Somebody") learned from a Black American singer he called "Lemon" Curtis and for whom he reserved special praise.[34] There were seven other informants. In all, these were a set of what might be called transatlantic retired sailors of the 1870s–1880s.

Doerflinger's information from personal sources was supplemented by half a dozen chanties from James Williams' article of 1909, three from the privately-held manuscript of 1880s sailor Nathaniel Silsbee, and another from an 1860s sea journal. Unfortunately, several of Doerflinger's recordings got damaged and did not survive after their transcription.[35]

Among other collecting work in this era the following products are of note. There are number of recordings in the Library of Congress, some of which were released commercially in the LP collection *American Sea Songs and Shanties*. On this one can hear the slow and deliberate tempo of authentic singers, and four of the tracks actually contain a couple men joining in the choruses. Various fieldworkers recorded Noble B. Brown (1946, Wisconsin) and Leighton Robinson (1939, 1951, California). Print collections from Nova Scotia that include a few chanties were made by folklorists W. Roy MacKenzie (1928) and Helen Creighton (1932). And inland waters collections were made from the sailors on the Great Lakes by University of Michigan Literature Professor Ivan H. Walton (1930s–50s)[36] and from the steamboat roustabouts on the Ohio River by Mary Wheeler (1944).

In sum, discussants in this layer furnished substantial primary source material for the study of chanties. Most significant are the recordings they made, on which one can hear people who actually sang the chanties in their professional work. As valuable as these recordings are, however, there are some potential issues of which to be aware. The recordings of the deepwater sailors who were old enough to have experienced chanties in their earliest years tend also to be the *oldest* recordings, which are very brief and of poorer quality. The recordings often skip and it is difficult to make out lyrics. One is also left to wonder if, at their age, the men were singing the songs anything like they would have when they were young[37]—not to mention how singing while seated alone with an observing folklorist may have altered the performance. In terms of sample, the focus on White men leaves us with only a partial view of chanty style as filtered through a particular perspective. At best it is like studying records by Mick Jagger and Robert Plant to learn about the Delta blues. The recordings of African-American and Caribbean singers, on the other hand, are quite good in quality and realism, but suffer from some poor contextualization and haphazard cataloging.

As for the perspectives of the collectors from this layer, there are several. Gordon, who did arguably the most evenly spread collecting amongst (presumably) White sailors and Black work-singers, believed chanties were related to African-American music yet suggested that the sailors had influenced the Black non-sailors. Carpenter, though an American, mainly explored the repertoire of British singers. This repertoire, perhaps unexpectedly for Carpenter, pointed to African-American origins. Lomax recorded both White and Black singers' work-song repertories, yet never seemed to make any special connection, having a preformed idea of what the chanty repertoire was, which, by the 1960s when he was going through the American South and the Caribbean, may have been influenced by his consciousness of the Folk Revival. Lastly, Doerflinger worked with men who were largely based in a "transatlantic" world, with less experience in the South and the Caribbean. He favored the idea of chanties being originally something basically English, which, in a certain time period, received a notable infusion of influence from Black sources.

Unlike Gordon, Carpenter, and Lomax, Doerflinger was very well-read in the published sources—especially those that had flourished since the mid-1920s—and their patterns and narratives had a distinct influence on his narrative.

Key works

1923　Carr Laughton, "Shantying and Shanties," *The Mariner's Mirror* (London)
1927　Gordon, "Folk Songs of America: Work Chanteys," *New York Times*
1927　Eckstorm and Smyth, *Minstrelsy of Maine: Folk-songs and Ballads of the Woods and the Coast* (Boston)
1928　MacKenzie, *Ballads and Sea Songs from Nova Scotia* (Cambridge, MA)
1929　Carpenter, "Forecastle Songs and Chanties," (PhD diss., Harvard)
1932　Creighton, *Songs and Ballads from Nova Scotia* (Toronto)
1938　Carpenter, "Chanteys in the Age of Sail," *New York Times*
1931　Carpenter, "Lusty Chanteys from Long-dead Ships," *New York Times*
1931　Carpenter, "Life Before the Mast: A Chantey Log," *New York Times*
1931　Carpenter, "Chanteys that 'Blow the Man Down'," *New York Times*
1935　Lomax, recordings in the Bahamas
1939　Lomax, recordings of Richard Maitland (New York)
1942　Parrish, *Slave Songs of the Georgia Sea Islands* (New York)
1944　Wheeler, *Steamboatin' Days: Folk Songs of the River Packet Era* (Baton Rouge)
1951　Doerflinger, *Shantymen and Shantyboys: Songs of the Sailor and Lumberman* (New York) [Revised, 1990]
1955　Lomax, recordings of Albert Rasmussen (London)
1959　Lomax, recordings of Georgia Sea Island Singers (St. Simons Island)
1960　Lomax, recordings of Bright Light Quartet (Lancaster County, Virginia)
1962　Lomax, recordings in the Caribbean

Notes for chapter 6

1　L. G. Carr Laughton, "Shantying and Shanties [part one]," *The Mariner's Mirror* 9.2 (1923): 48.
2　Recall Kidson's utter confusion at what to make of the copious mention of American places and the paucity of European places in chanty lyrics.
3　Carr Laughton, "Shantying and Shanties [part one]," 50.
4　Ibid., 50.
5　Ibid., 51.
6　L. G. Carr Laughton, "Shantying and Shanties [part two]," *The Mariner's Mirror* 9.3 (1923): 72.
7　Hugill, *Shanties from the Seven Seas*, 12.
8　Carr Laughton, "Shantying and Shanties [part two]," 70.
9　Ibid., 74.

10 Deborah G. Kodish, "Introduction," in liner notes of *"Folk-songs of America": The Robert Winslow Gordon Collection, 1922–1932*, ed. Neil V. Rosenberg and Deborah G. Kodish (Library of Congress, 1978), 6.

11 Ibid., 6.

12 Ibid., 10.

13 Ibid., 11.

14 A few of Gordon's recordings were commercially released on an LP, *"Folk-songs of America": The Robert Winslow Gordon Collection, 1922–1932* (Library of Congress, 1978).

15 Robert Winslow Gordon, "Folk Songs of America: Work Chanteys," *New York Times*, January 16, 1927, 7.

16 Robert Winslow Gordon, "Folk Songs of America: A Hunt on Hidden Trails," *New York Times*, January 2, 1927, 3.

17 Lydia Parrish, *Slave Songs of the Georgia Sea Islands* (New York: Creative Age Press, 1942), 197.

18 Alan Jabbour and Julia C. Bishop, "The James Madison Carpenter Collection," *Folk Music Journal* 7.4 (1998): 399.

19 Ibid., 399.

20 See: Robert Young Walser, "'Here We Come Home in a Leaky Ship!': The Shanty Collection of James Madison Carpenter," *Folk Music Journal* 7.4 (1998).

21 Julia C. Bishop, "'Dr Carpenter from the Harvard College in America': An Introduction to James Madison Carpenter and his Collection," *Folk Music Journal* 7.4 (1998): 404.

22 This is my own tally.

23 Walser, "'Here We Come Home…'," 472.

24 Walser points out, likewise, that it gives us a glimpse of only a portion of the chanty tradition. "'Here We Come Home…'," 474.

25 James Madison Carpenter, "Lusty Chanteys from Long-dead Ships," *New York Times*, July 12, 1931, 13.

26 James Madison Carpenter, "Chanteys in the Age of Sail," *New York Times*, October 30, 1938.

27 Carpenter, "Lusty Chanteys," 13.

28 See: Alan Lomax, *Bahamas 1935—Chanteys and Anthems from Andros and Cat Island* (Rounder, 1999).

29 See: Bessie Jones and the Georgia Sea Island Singers, *Georgia Sea Island Songs* (liner notes by A. Lomax) (New World, 1977).

30 *American Sea Songs & Shanties*, ed. Duncan Emrich (Rounder, 2004).

31 William Main Doerflinger, *Songs of the Sailor and Lumberman* (Glenwood, IL: Meyerbooks, 1990), 91–3.

32 Ibid., 96–7.

33 Ibid., 98.

34 Ibid., 45–7.

35 Stephen D. Winick, "'Sung with Gusto by the Men': A Unique Recording of 'The Leaving of Liverpool' in the AFC Archive," *Folklife Center News* 30.3/4 (2008): 6.

36 Ivan H. Walton with Joe Grimm, *Windjammers: Songs of the Great Lakes Sailors* (Detroit: Wayne State University, 2002).

37 Hugill asserted that the slow tempo of many of these singers was not, in fact, reflect reality as he experienced it (*Bosun's Locker*, 30). This leaves us to wonder whether the style of these singers was not due to some factor of difference such as their advanced ages.

VII — THE FINAL SEAL: STAN HUGILL

The name of Stan Hugill (1906–1992) is synonymous with chanties. Not only was Hugill a merchant sailor in some of Britain's last sailing vessels, in which chanties were sometimes sung—or at least remembered—he took an explicit academic interest in the genre. This meant that while chanties had long been on their way out by the time Hugill sailed in the 1920s and '30s, he had the presence of mind to ask older shipmates for the chanties they learned in earlier years. Born to a seafaring family in Hoylake, Cheshire (near Liverpool), Hugill's pedigree was about as good as one could wish for his generation. So when, as he relates, Hugill was laid up with an injury and away from his post-seaman job as an instructor of youngsters at the Outward Bound Sea School at Aberdovey, an opportunity arose to combine his experience and knowledge in a published collection.

Hugill's *Shanties from the Seven Seas* (1961) has become one of the most celebrated and influential volumes on chanties. To a great extent, *Shanties from the Seven Seas* is considered the last word on chanties and the first stop as a reference for chanty enthusiasts. So while Hugill's sea experience earned him the moniker "The Last Shantyman," he was also one of the last original chanty *collectors*. The book's seemingly authoritative position is bolstered by the personal image of its author. In contrast to many of the academic folklorists who had collected chanties before him, Hugill possessed the look (including queue, beard, tattoos, and a muscular frame) and pedigree of an old-time sailor. Importantly, he was also able to actually *perform* the songs from his collection.

In the process of writing the book, Hugill began to engage with the maritime music revival, first in the U.K., and eventually became its central figure. Maritime scholar Stuart Frank, a past director of the chanty programs and Sea Music Festivals that began at Mystic Seaport in the 1970s, relates how, at the age of 70, Hugill participated in the OpSail event for America's Bicentennial in 1976, after which his fame began to spread there.[1] Frank explains that in 1977 the Maine Maritime Museum then brought Hugill to the States to lecture and tour the Northeast. "From those auspicious beginnings—Stan's first forays into America since deepwater days—there gradually arose a groundswell of chanteying nationwide."[2] By that time, many of the chanties the American audiences knew had been greatly influenced by versions in Hugill's book. A generation of maritime music enthusiasts saw the chanties of their imagination embodied in a near perfect figure—whose occasional flaws made him all the more endearing according to the stereotype of a sailor's propensity to spin yarns and impetuously go where a more cautious academic scholar would not. To reiterate: *Shanties from the Seven Seas* is regarded not just for its voluminous content, but also in relation to the persona of its author. This all created a multi-layered phenomenon of the perception of authenticity. To mix metaphors, Hugill's book became the "Bible" of late 20th-century chanty enthusiasts, and as a chanty authority Hugill himself was, like Muhammad, the "seal" of the Prophets.

Shipboard Work-songs and Songs Used as Work-songs
from the Great Days of Sail
—The subtitle of Hugill's magnum opus, 1961

Because of the great influence of *Shanties from the Seven Seas*, it is vital to assess both its content and how it was put together. Due to Hugill's methodology and the work's chronological position, it became the largest collection of its time. Hugill aimed to be as inclusive as possible—to account for and to present, if sometimes only in fragments, any and all items of chanty repertoire that he was able to find. Any song that he had heard or read being attested as having been ever "used as a shanty" was included—even if that song was not generally known as a chanty or its use as a chanty was rare and incidental. Hugill readily included more recently popular songs that evidently were not sung until after the chanty genre was experiencing decline, but which were extant when Hugill sailed. He also culled from the major collections of non-English-language sailor work-songs. A great number of the items in the collection are drawn from prior sources and many others are a combination of prior published material *mixed in with* material he had learned. The latter such composites should be read as idealistic presentations conceived at the time of publication rather than as a record of one sailor's experiences at sea. It may also be noted in passing that many of the tune notations in *Shanties* have errors.[3] (This can be seen from both the difference in Hugill's performances from the text and in certain musical figures that simply do not make sense.) Unfortunately, this leads to some reservation, in the absence of other versions to compare, about the notational accuracy of the original items.

Perhaps the most valuable parts of the work for scholars are the entirely original items as well as versions of familiar items that Hugill drew from his experience. These can often be identified by the fact that they do not appear in any of the works in Hugill's bibliography. Hugill's sea experience included voyages to the Windward Islands of the Caribbean and significant interactions with West Indian seamen. Among those he identifies, a chief contributor was a shipmate he calls Harding, "The Barbadian Barbarian." Some 38 chanties in the collection are attributed to Harding—so many that in today's custom one might be tempted to credit Harding as a sort of co-author. Similar contributors were "Harry Lauder" and "Tobago Smith."[4]

The result of Hugill's sources and methods, the combination of disparate works and collapsing of time periods, is a varied portrait of the genre, highlighting its maximum diversity without, however, giving a focused sense of what songs were most common during the heyday of chanties or in latter eras. Hugill's practice of liberally culling from all major prior works, *in combination with* original material from his own field experiences, makes it a handy sourcebook of ideas for performers, but a difficult work to assess in terms of historical accuracy. Further, because Hugill had read most of the prior available writing of folklorists, his background statements on the items and even his choice of what new lyrics to include incidentally, both reveal and contribute to a certain bias that was wholly different from a relatively uninfluenced writer like Bullen.

> *...I find it too dogmatic to state that this shanty is a*
> *capstan or that a halyard song.*

Hugill's method of organizing the songs is unusual and also contributes to a certain view of the genre that limits its use as a scholarly source. As opposed to the method established in earlier writing of presenting the chanties under categories of working tasks, Hugill used a method of "family tree" organization. The rationale for this was that many chanties were used for more than one task, so it would be artificial to file them in only one task-related category. I think the issue this presents is exaggerated; earlier seaman authors did not find this to be a problem, though they acknowledged the same issue of overlap. Perhaps they were mainly writing only from their own experiences, or at least giving authority to their own experiences. Yet Hugill was faced with gathering sources with different claims. The "family tree" method comes off as a rambling narrative that moves from one chanty to the next based on their containing shared words, like "Johnny" or "Ranzo." However, as many of these words had become common tropes in chantymen's language, grouping them together on this basis often appears arbitrary. The method emphases the focus on text that one finds in some Folklore scholarship.

The impression that *Shanties from the Seven Seas* gives from the content of its chanties and how they have been organized differs from the impression one might get from a reading of 19th-century and other primary sources. Bullen's collection provides an excellent foil. One will recall that Bullen was adamant that his collection should include only those songs that he considered firmly centered as work-songs. The majority of these appear to be African-American in origin. Yet Hugill included very many songs that could be used as work-songs—that may have been used for work even if on just one occasion. These are more or less all songs used for *heaving* tasks. The hauling chanties were of a particular form that was specific to the genre, whereas during heaving tasks, especially the continuous pumping or marching around the capstan, a wide range of styles could be adopted. Songs that were better known as forebitters or entertainment songs of the sea and shore, by dint of some occurrence of being sung at the capstan, become "chanties" within the context of Hugill's work. At the same time, such songs, which often had a longer and consistent narrative and which came from many national traditions, became canonized. One result is that Revival performers, who were not working whilst singing, tended to gravitate towards these songs; they provided more interest and cohesiveness in the context of entertainment, and hauling songs were avoided. Such songs began to appear to characterize the chanty genre—after all, the "authority" on chanties had classed them as such. Another result is that, because these songs were often not of the African-American work-song style, there appeared to be ample evidence to consider European traditional songs and ballads as part of the makeup of the genre. This further enables the elision of "sea shanty" with "sea song" and bolsters the sense that the chanty repertoire is significantly English (or, alternately, broadly international) in its origins.

If we are to analyze the content of Hugill's chanties, based on an assessment of the likely cultural origins of each song, little more than 15% conservatively, or at most liberal estimate 30%, could be called distinctly "English" in origin. If one further considers only the songs that might be regarded as "genuine" chanties (primary work-songs), and excludes those entertainment songs that were only seldom put to use for labor tasks as a secondary purpose, the percentage of "English" chanties becomes quite low indeed. Over a third of the chanty items in the text (over half, in the abridged edition, which omits most foreign-language songs) reflect explicit African-American origins.[5] Now, one may quarrel with my assessment of the cultural origins of individual items, and it would take too much discussion to present the argument for each one. If one accepts at least that the "English" chanties make up a minority of the repertoire, the point can be made that the repertoire items that have been emphasized in Revival performances have tended to be drawn *disproportionately*, from the "English" section of the repertoire. It may be noted that Hugill himself was evidently uncomfortable singing the more obviously culturally "Black" songs,[6] resulting in his performances being less representative of the cultural breadth of the repertoire than is in evidence in his publications.

In not wishing to be "dogmatic," Hugill could be accused of having been altogether too loose about classifying the repertoire, leaving it open to tacit assumptions by his readers.

It is fairly obvious that the wharves of Mobile and
such places were the meeting ground of white men's songs
and shanties and Negro songs and work-songs.

While Hugill's methods of organization and selection may unintentionally give undue weight to English culture, this is not the case with his comments in the book's introduction. Like many sailor writers of earlier times and in contrast to his lay contemporaries, Hugill had significant formative experiences with Black chantymen. This leads him to make direct statements about this influence, as well.

> I am rather inclined to think that Negro shanties or shanties developed from Negro songs were more common about this period than the authorities seem to suggest.[7]

Of all the sources for chanties, indeed, Hugill has perhaps the most to say about the Afro-American, especially those from the West Indies, where he had sailed, and whose people he thought may have produced the greater number of chanties.[8] As to who performed chanties he makes frequent reference to the idea of so-called "checkerboard crews" in which one watch was Black and the other White. Overall, Hugill made no attempt to discount the contribution of African-American work-songs, though his interest in chanties as an English, Liverpool man with experience among Northern European seamen, meant that he was sure to emphasize those aspects as well.

The history of the development of the chanty genre that Hugill presents is quite reasonable. On the back of Doerflinger's discussion, he states that chanties probably developed more aboard American ships, but follows that these ships were manned with many crew from Britain, Ireland, and Scandinavia.[9] In considering the formidable evidence of chanty development in the Gulf

Ports, he calls Mobile, Alabama a "shanty mart" where European sailors who came to work brought their chanties and went away with new songs influenced by the local African-Americans.[10] Overall, the emphasis is on an idea that would prove popular: that chanties were eminently international, forged from the cultural influences and repertoire of many nations and at many times. Readers would take from this whatever emphasis they wanted, to include their own identities into the chanty Revival, even while the effect of the rest of the presentation and Hugill's performances (as an embodiment of the tradition) tended to reserve the European as the default basis.

Hugill was not a trained folklorist or historian, though he did make an honest effort to find and review a good range of sources. In *Shanties from the Seven Seas*, he often wrestles with bits of information in the presentation of songs, offering conclusions but leaving the verdict up to the reader. So although the book is a "popular" collection, it is by no means concise and perhaps includes *too much* information for some audiences. As the maritime music movement developed, Hugill was called upon to provide further popular collections of a more focused nature. His *Shanties and Sailors' Songs* (1969) was a more succinct presentation of some of the earlier material, also including some updates from new revelations.[11] The tighter presentation, however, means that items are not problematized; Hugill's speculations appear positive. For example, regarding the chanty "John Kanaka," in his earlier work Hugill suggested, with room for doubt, that the song emanated from a body of Polynesian songs learned by Anglophone sailors.[12] However, over the years this rare item became one of Hugill's signature songs, replete with a simplified accompanying narrative, and in his later work he stated positively and grandiosely that it "the only known representative of a sizeable group of Anglicized Polynesian work-songs…"[13] This trend of narrative-building and simplification of evidence continued with another book, *Songs of the Sea* (1977), which is much more like a song-book than an academic volume. Each item it presents, and the information about it, appears to look more standardized.

Works of Stan Hugill

1961   *Shanties from the Seven Seas: Shipboard Work-songs and Songs Used as Work-songs from the Great Days of Sail.* [Republished, abridged, 1994]

1962–1973 "The Bosun's Locker" [regular column], *Spin* (Liverpool)

1969   *Shanties and Sailors' Songs*

1977   *Songs of the Sea*

Notes for chapter 7

1 Stan Hugill, *Shanties from the Seven Seas: Shipboard Work-songs and Songs Used as Work-songs from the Great Days of Sail*, abridged edition (Mystic, CT: Mystic Seaport, 1994), xx.

2 Ibid., xx.

3 Hugill evidently had little facility with music notation; the melodies for his book were taken down by his brother, Harold.

4 By my count, Hugill explicitly ascribes 54 of his chanties, or about 17% of them, to West Indian informants.

5 The first percentage reflects the original edition (Routledge and Kegan Paul, 1961), while the second reflects the abridged edition (Mystic Seaport, 1994). An explanation of the methodology of this reckoning is in order. The original edition of Hugill's text contained some one hundred unique items more than the abridged text. These were largely non-English language songs that Hugill culled from Scandinavian, German, and French works. Their presence skews the percentages accordingly, so the abridged text may give a more realistic picture of the *Anglophone* repertoire. My method of counting the number of chanties demanded that I decide what constituted a distinct item. I counted those songs for which both a unique text and melody were given, along with a title heading. Mere lyrical variations, so far as the lyrics of all chanties were quite variable, were not counted as distinct items, nor were songs explicitly stated to be non-chanties. Many songs that were most of the time treated as forebitters but which, on the basis of a cited source, were sometimes said to be "used as chanties," *were* nonetheless counted. In the unabridged edition I counted 323 chanty items (among 416 variants) and in the abridged edition I counted 222 chanty items (out of 274 variants). Of these, the chanties I considered to be of significantly Black American and Caribbean origin numbered 119 (unabridged). Note also that some 49 chanties in the text were those that I considered to be of "indeterminate" origin, having not enough information to sway my opinion (and no supporting comment by Hugill) as to what tradition contributed mostly to their origins. These are mainly chanties that, although structured on the African-American based paradigm of work-song, are probably later products of multi-ethnic crews, the chanty-building paradigm having been well assimilated.

6 Jerry Bryant, personal communication, March 2009.

7 Hugill, *Shanties from the Seven Seas* (1961), 10.

8 Ibid., 8.

9 Ibid., 11.

10 Ibid., 17.

11 From 1962 to 1973, Hugill wrote a regular column called "The Bosun's Locker" for the Liverpool-based folk music periodical *Spin*, in which he sometimes brought in newly discovered findings. These were later gathered in the volume *The Bosun's Locker* (2006).

12 Hugill, *Shanties from the Seven Seas* (1961), 288.

13 Stan Hugill, *Shanties and Sailors' Songs* (New York: Praeger, 1969), 187.

VIII — POST-HUGILL STUDIES (1960s–2010s)

Since Stan Hugill's entry—that is to say, for over fifty years—little original has been published about the deepwater chanty repertoire. That ground appears to be considered more or less covered; so much faith is put in Hugill's work that many consider his chanties impeccably authentic and the information eminently quotable. That is to say, it is authentic *enough*. Hugill's discourse is filled with intentional irony, well tuned to the demographics of his audience, which promotes an attitude of distrust towards those who claim authenticity and ascribes authenticity to those who spin yarns. Insiders are, by definition, authentic, and Hugill made a second career out of being The Insider. To know chanties—all you *really* need to know about chanties—or so it would seem, is to know Hugill's work.[1] I have yet to see anything in print that really challenges Hugill, and it is typical for writers to cite him without evidently checking his sources. And while it is true that some critical readers have no problem seeing Hugill as fallible, their criticism is easily outweighed by those who appeal to authority when citing Hugill's statements.

With the assumption in place that Hugill's work was solid, the only place it would seem work could go in the post-Hugill era (i.e. the late twentieth century) was to find more material. And yet it is true that the time of deepwater singers was over, and few remembered anything new. New things would have to be discovered beyond, geographically or in text, what the discourse had produced as the "standard" repertoire. The seekers in this area might be grouped, for the purpose of the present survey, as Late Folklorists. Texts and their interpretation remain primary for them.

Still others have built on the study of chanties by viewing the genre's history through different lenses. Representing the fields ethnomusicology and history, these scholars tend to be interested in the broader context of chanty-singing.

> *Many have lamented the death of sea shantying,*
> *but the practice is far from dead.*
> —Roger Abrahams, 1974

One of the new repertoire areas for collecting was so-called Caribbean chanties, a sphere in which chanty-singing was still being or recently had been practiced. Whereas in one sense the chanty repertoire generally might be argued to be global in that global seafarers spread it, it is also reasonable to suppose some items of repertoire were particular to certain spheres of travel or work. So far as maritime workers continued to sing chanties in the Caribbean islands in the twentieth century, and a good number of these songs were not or not well-represented in the literature focused on deepwater merchant sailing, a sphere of "Caribbean chanties" seems justified.

Folklorist Roger Abrahams (1933–) found himself working on the islands of Nevis, St. Vincent, and Tobago in the early 1960s. (Alan Lomax had covered some of the same ground in Nevis at the same time.) At this time Abrahams was familiar with the recently released volumes by Hugill and Harlow.[2] In fact, he had been a participant in Folk Revival activities and had appeared on a sea music album.[3] The result of this was the small but important volume, the work of one of the twentieth century's distinguished professors of Folklore: *Deep the Water, Shallow the Shore* (1974).

Abrahams characterizes chanties as occupying the space where Afro-Americans and Euro-Americans worked together, without attempting to "solve the problem of origins."[4] However, years later and after the publication of his book about corn-shucking songs of the American South,[5] he drew a stronger connection to the African in noting the wide spread of songs of the chanty type throughout African America.[6] Abrahams notes that the chanty song type was once associated by Euro-American observers with African-Americans,[7] though he says it was especially associated with West Indians and wonders why many earlier authors did not note this.[8] Abrahams notes that the use of chanties was everywhere in the Caribbean, but for other tasks not limited to ship-board work.

Also presenting Caribbean chanties, but without much background information or discussion (and with a rather unsatisfactory presentation of items) was folklorist Horace Beck. The discussion comes in a chapter of Beck's volume *Folklore and the Sea* (1973), which had been published prior to Abrahams' work. It was the latter work that most endured however, and inspired the invitation of some of Abrahams' informants, under the banner of "The Barouallie Whalers," to Mystic Seaport in 2002. Continued interest led ex-Seaport Chanteyman Dan Lanier and native St. Vincentian, Vincent Reid, to continue facilitating outside interactions with the Whalers and their tradition.[9]

While not the subject of a major publication, the "chanteys" of menhaden fishermen (e.g. as recorded by Lomax earlier) received renewed interest after Mystic Seaport invited the Menhaden Chanteymen of Beaufort, North Carolina to perform in 1991.[10] In the same year, a group of retired menhaden fishermen from Virginia, whose careers spanned the 1930s–1980s, came together to perform under the name Northern Neck Chantey Singers.[11]

> *...though the end of the deepwater sailing ship work*
> *song tradition may reasonably be placed in the 1920s, that*
> *does not mark the end of this repertoire's use as work song.*
> —Bob Walser, 1995

Perhaps the most significant new discourse around chanties at the end of the twentieth century was inspired by the rediscovery of J. M. Carpenter's collection. A research team under the auspices of the Elphinstone Institute at the University of Aberdeen started working on a critical edition of the collection in some form in the 1990s. They cataloged the items in the collection by 2003 and put it on-line,[12] allowing some glimpse into its contents for those who cannot visit the Library of Congress. The critical edition will be published by the University of Mississippi Press,[13] and the Library of Congress has arranged to put the digitized Carpenter Collection on-line by incorporating it into *The Full English* digital archive.[14] Former Mystic Seaport Chanteyman and ethnomusicology Ph.D. Bob Walser has been in charge of the sailor songs component, on which he first gave a published report in 1998.[15] Enthusiasts with access to parts of the Collection have been inspired to learn some of the chanties that it holds, and to informally debate the history of some of the more obscure items. Walser himself, an active participant in the Sea Music subculture, has helped to introduce some of the previously unfamiliar chanties into the Revival repertoire.[16]

If Carpenter's work, which made little impact on the course chanty-related discourse when it first appeared (it was not accessed by the Middle Folklorists and Hugill), came to influence 21st-century discussions, Walser's own insights from studying Carpenter have remained at low profile (at least in their written form). Walser's Master's thesis (1995) considered the received image of the chanty repertoire. It found that the views of the sailors whose singing was documented, of the collectors of those songs, and of subsequent editors had contributed to a notably limited image of the genre.[17] In the wake of the work of Late Folklorists expanding the area of collection to more recent African-American practices, Walser critiqued the narrative of the death of chanty-singing that had so influenced collection and revival efforts of the early twentieth century. As I put it in my own work, the conventional history of chanties is perhaps better specified to be the history of *White people's engage-*

ment with chanties. Walser writes that chanties "should be seen both as arising from and devolving to forms of black work song."[18]

Another alum of Mystic Seaport is Stuart Frank, who, even if he had written nothing about chanties, could be considered an essential contributor to oral discourse. Having organized music programs at the Seaport throughout the 1970s, Frank was instrumental in bringing Stan Hugill to eastern American audiences. Though he has not created a volume to advance a particular thesis about chanties, as Director of the Kendall Whaling Museum, Frank brought to light numerous new pieces of evidence from manuscript sources like sailors' journals. Frank's vision of the history of chanties appears to have developed over the years, being first greatly under the influence of Hugill yet by 2000 making the decidedly non-Hugillian remark that, "The practice of chanteying on shipboard is descended from West African traditional work-songs..."[19]

Winner of the Alan Merriam Prize, an annual recognition of a distinguished monograph in ethnomusicology, *Hawaiian Music in Motion* by Revell Carr (2014) is poised to bring discourse on chanties to a new sphere. Yet another alumnus of Mystic Seaport's program, as well as a former Ranger at San Francisco Maritime National Historic Park, Carr built upon his early experiences in the Sea Music scene to research the in- and outflows of musical culture across the Hawaiian Islands. Having drawn some inspiration from Hugill's tantalizing presentation of "John Kanaka" as a representative of Polynesian-style chanties, Carr weaves the topic into this study of intercultural exchange to suggest both the influence of chanties on Hawaiian popular music and a contribution of Kanaka sailors to the chanty genre. He writes, "While most sea music scholars have described chanteys as a hybrid of European and African work song traditions, with primarily Anglo-Irish origins, I present evidence that Hawaiian sailors had a significant role in the development of chantey singing as it came to be known in the nineteenth century."[20] It is true that Anglo-Celtic and African-American characteristics are by far most attributed to the genre, and for good reason. It was Hugill who most emphasized a multiplicity of cultural influences, including Pacific Island culture,[21] yet offered little evidence to make the case. Not so much departing from past narrative as expanding the global narrative of chanties in the wake of Hugill, Carr uses the idea of multifarious influences to open a space to talk about Hawaiian influence. I have previously referred to this as a "postmodern" approach in which the specific sites of particular importance in prior chanty history—the Mobile Bays, with their interactions between Black stevedores and White mariners—find their weight diminished by a free-floating, around-the-world view of what Carr calls "the unique musical culture of the sea."[22] There is no doubt, however, that a perspective on chanties from the vantage of Hawaiian musical history is one way of approaching the subject fresh.

My own project began in 2008, not to discover new chanties, but rather to overhaul the existing repertoire. As an ethnomusicologist who had practiced oral history among marginalized communities in South Asia, I was skeptical of the accuracy of current dominant discourses and I wondered how the chanties I learned in younger days would hold up to critical inquiry. I decided to try to view historical chanty-singing with fewer assumptions, as an ethnomusicologist views an unfamiliar music-culture. The project began with a close reading of Hugill's magnum opus, and has continued in a hermeneutic fashion with the idea that a regular return to the same material, after time away looking at contrasting sources, might each time yield new insights. The reading was approached in a novel way: that of learning (including by memory) all of the known items in the chanty repertoire, so as to both address their practical challenges and to simulate a sort of organic learning experience. I eventually began to compile a comprehensive bibliography, in this process working in dialogue with some individuals on the Internet discussion board, *The Mudcat Café*.[23] I use a broad array of sources outside of conventional frames of reference (e.g. "the sea," "sailors' songs," "folk music," "work-songs") to view the chanty genre from a subaltern vantage. These include primary sources like journals, periodicals, and travelogues dealing especially with slave life and African-American vernacular culture. Presenting this perspective has necessitated much ground clearing and thus required deconstruction of the knowledge that has been produced.[24]

There is yet much to be said about the topic of chanties, and digital archives and increased accessibility of sources facilitate further study even of familiar items and concepts. Carpenter's, Gordon's and Lomax's recordings can be overhauled for starters. Most new insight, however, will not be found in sources categorized under such subject headings as "sailing ships" or "music." The evidence is hidden among disparate sources being looked at by social historians focusing on the lives of working people in specific locales during the nineteenth to twentieth centuries.[25] When these scholars run across information important to chanty history, one would hope they recognize its importance and share the references with chanty scholars. Yet that is only possible once the writing of chanty-focused scholars makes it known that we are *interested* in references beyond the frame fixed by so many of the go-to works of the last century. Today's researchers need a reference work other than

Hugill, and a critical guide to literature on chanties that has been colored by romantic notions of music, seafaring, and folk-song.

Noted works

1973   Beck, *Folklore and the Sea* (Mystic, CT)

1974   Abrahams, *Deep The Water, Shallow the Shore* (Austin)

1995   Walser, "The Shantyman's Canon" (MA thesis, Univ. of Wisconsin, Madison)

2000   Frank, *Sea Chanteys and Sailors' Songs* (Sharon, MA)

2007   Lanier and Reid. "Whalers' Shanties of Barouallie, St. Vincent," *International Journal of Intangible Heritage* (Seoul)

2014   Schreffler, "Twentieth-Century Editors and the Re-envisioning of Chanties: A Case Study of 'Lowlands'" (Buzzards Bay, MA)

2014   Carr, *Hawaiian Music in Motion* (Urbana)

Notes for chapter 8

1   By way of illustration: A user at *Mudcat.org*, on the subject of spellings of the term chanty, writes,

   If 'shanty' was good enough for Stan Hugill, it's good enough for me. <http://awe.mudcat.org/thread.cfm?threadid=125224&page=2#2771558>

   The author at *Worksongs.org* writes, in reference to the chanty, "One More Day":

   It's authentic. As I said, this one comes from the great collection of simple call-and-response songs that were used on ships to help get through hard work on long journeys. If Stan Hugill sang it, it's the real deal. <http://www.worksongs.org/blog/2013/03/09/yww-003-one-more-day>

2   Roger D. Abrahams, Review of *Chanteying Aboard American Ships*, Frederick Pease Harlow, Western Folklore 22.3 (1963): 219.

3   Paul Clayton and the Foc'sle Singers, *Foc'sle Songs and Shanties* (Folkways, 1959).

4   Roger D. Abrahams, *Deep The Water, Shallow the Shore* (Mystic, CT: Mystic Seaport Museum, 2002), xvii.

5   Singing the Master: *The Emergence of African American Culture in the Plantation South* (New York: Pantheon, 1992).

6   Abrahams, *Deep the Water*, xiii.

7   Ibid., xvii.

8   Ibid., 9–10.

9   Daniel Lanier and Vincent Reid, "Whalers' Shanties of Barouallie, St. Vincent: Observations on the Nature, Decline and Revival of a Unique Caribbean Maritime Tradition," *International Journal of Intangible Heritage* 2 (2007).

10 The Seaport's festival coordinator, Geoff Kaufman, had first heard the group on an NPR broadcast in 1989. Carr, "Interpreted Authenticity," 4.

11 Harold Anderson, "Menhaden Chanteys: An African American Maritime Legacy," *Maryland Marine Notes* 18.1 (2000).

12 The catalog is hosted by the University of Sheffield at: <http://www.hrionline.ac.uk/carpenter/>.

13 <http://www.abdn.ac.uk/elphinstone/carpenter/elements/>

14 <http://www.vwml.org.uk/search/search-full-english#>

15 Walser, "'Here We Come Home…'."

16 Walser has offered his renditions of Carpenter's collected chanties on several albums: When Our Ship Comes Home (1999), Landlocked (2002), and Outward Bound on the J.M. Carpenter (2010).

17 Robert Young Walser, "The Shantyman's Canon," MA thesis (Univ. of Wisconsin, Madison, 1995), 138139.

18 Walser, "Shantyman's Canon," 135.

19 Stuart M. Frank, *Sea Chanteys and Sailors' Songs: An Introduction for Singers and Performers, and a Guide for Teachers and Group Leaders* (Sharon, MA: The Kendall Whaling Museum, 2000), 1.

20 James Revell Carr, *Hawaiian Music in Motion: Mariners, Missionaries, and Minstrels* (Urbana: University of Illinois, 2014), 12.

21 Hugill, Shanties from the Seven Seas, 19–20.

22 Ibid., 95.

23 These include, but are no means limited to Steve Gardham, Jonathan Lighter, and John Minear.

24 See e.g.: Schreffler, "Twentieth Century Editors."

25 For example, David Cecelski and Michael Thompson, while not working on chanties, uncovered notable references to chanty-singing while conducting research on workers in North Carolina and South Carolina.

CONCLUDING NOTE

The writing on chanties was mostly work researched and published at a time when the practical use of chanties was in sharp decline or had disappeared entirely from the possible view of its authors. Some of it gives us a precious window into what chanties were like in their deepwater heyday. Other parts of it, due to bias, lack of due diligence, or simple human error mislead us or obscure the view. Which parts are which? Such is the problematic nature of discourse that takes place long after events and between people distanced from their experience. Hence the historian's preference for contemporary, primary sources! Still, how can we discover, select, and interpret those sources without the influence of current discourse? We cannot escape the fact that what are generally viewed to be the age, the cultural origins, and the core repertoire of chanties, along with many other finer details, developed through this discourse in the manner of a sort of "telephone game."

Factors contributing to this development included the very nature of the print medium itself: its customary need for standard texts, its legitimizing authority, its reifying effect, and the tendency of writers to look to previous writers. All this went into creating a rather independent body of written, as opposed to oral, lore. Each text influenced how following writers would approach the topic, creating models and circumscribing the potential material for consideration.

The emergence of the academic field of Folklore was another factor, as discussants in the early days of the field were often concerned with preservation, not so much of evidence for future research, but rather of the traditions themselves. Folklore enthusiasts were inspired by an interest in the songs of their own national or ethnic traditions, which led them to look for items and characteristics in the genre that were most pertinent to these traditions, sometimes at the expense of others. Early Folklore's method demanded a somewhat reductive approach to songs, often focusing on key words as clues to origin, rather than viewing these elements as potentially free-floating or incidental. Because of their emphasis on these synchronic dimensions, little history was attempted by the Early Folklorists. Contemporary or recent data was instead compared to divine the past, with background researches being rather limited to the "obvious" sources—in this case, works about English sailors or English folk-songs. Even the rather evident source of minstrel songs, about which there would certainly be available texts, was ignored because these popular sources were not generally considered valuable to the concept of a folk "essence" that discussants sought to confirm. And so the resultant presentations, more selective than objective in their choice of repertoire, came to suggest a particular ethnically Anglo-British cast to the genre.

Although my survey has neglected to narrate the activities of so-called Revival performers, it must be noted that their presentations, during the first chanty boom in the 1920s and in the larger Folk Revival begun in the 1950s, contributed much more to these trends. In performing chanties, one appears to really *represent* them, to embody them, in a way that can have a powerful and convincing effect on audiences. Revival performers were mostly White and often oriented towards British and Irish heritage, so it was both their prerogative and, one might assume, natural inclination to focus on these components of the genre and to speak from these perspectives. At the same time, it made sense and, sometimes, was political good taste to avoid or alter material that spoke strongly from a Black voice.

So how has all this past discourse and these representations shaped current ideas about and presentations of chanties? What sort of people, what time period, or what ethos does a performance of chanties appear to represent? What should a performer be aiming for, in terms of style and selection of repertoire? Who will identify with the genre and who, perhaps, will feel alienated by or disinterested in it? How does what we believe about chanties suggest we interpret music history, as well as the non-musical aspects of history about which we believe music informs? And what do current beliefs about chanties suggest about how we should go about future research?

The answers depend on whom one asks. As for myself, one cannot have failed to noticed, in my foregoing narrative, regular remarks on race, chiefly focused on "White" and "Black" agents and social spheres. While such an emphasis and the simple binary distinction can be criticized, I believe that for such a broad overview as this, race is important enough a factor and the White/Black dichotomy sufficient to begin parsing the major issues that steer the discourse. While I acknowledge that race is of particular interest to my research, the commentary supplied by authors, noted above, is sufficient to argue that it was important to them, too. One might compare the broad history of Rock 'n' Roll in America, where the notion of these racial categories is inseparable from the music. And so my research aims to consider evidence that will sufficiently represent "both" races. For instance, I view the popular framing of chanties as only shipboard songs to be partly the result of the discourse of White authors who were inclined to focus on the context in which they encountered (or imagined) chanties sung by other White people: on the sea. Stevedores in the ports, however, must have sung far more chanties as they labored than seaman did, since the latter's heavy tasks were sporadic while the former's were continuous. The stevedores, however, were both less liable to be encountered by the authors of chanty discussions and more likely to be Black—disqualifying them as subjects of English "folk" research.

My experience tells me that much of the general public in both Britain and North America (among other places) tends to believe chanties in general originated in Britain, or at least chiefly among Britons. Some of the most pronounced outcomes of this perspective come in the anachronistic adopting of chanty repertoire by "pyrate" interpreters and Elizabethan players at Renaissance Faires. Such adaptors of the genre—who have just as much right to perform the repertoire as anyone else—seem to sing chanties largely because of their supposedly very English *nature*. Perhaps the assumption by some *Americans*, at least, is that if it is "White" and it is "old"—i.e. chanties as they have been presented in mainstream narratives—then it must be English. One could go on in speculating and providing anecdotes of why and how Britain enjoys a privileged place in the mass imagination of chanties, or why even people in America prefer to imagine *New England* as the necessary fount of chanty history. But *how* the discourse brought us here, at last, is not my concern so much as *what* the perception is. Even if we leave aside the more fanciful ideas about jig-like sea shanties, pirates, and jolly British tars, among those individuals more actively involved with chanty performance one may still note a strong bias towards White English culture as the sort of definitive source for chanties. So while individuals in today's atmosphere may accept a given chanty as "American" in use or content, its *ethnic* affiliation might be assumed to be White English—or else Irish.[1] In the main, those participating in this music scene are not professional scholars and they certainly have no reason to (pedantically, some might say) weigh the formative cultural influences on chanty-singing. Yet chanties often serve for them, among other functions, a cultural template with which they identify to some significant degree. By way of example, chanty-singer Walter "Salty Walt" Askew remembers growing up in a New York of the 1970s where discovering and emphasizing one's "roots" was encouraged. He discovered chanties in part through the process of focusing on his Scots-English heritage, although with time the growing idea of *American* heritage late in the century suggested other possibilities for interpreting the material, including highlighting the African-American contributions.[2]

Indeed, unlike music forms that are thought more broadly to be "American" and which lack particular associations with White Americans—e.g. Blues,

Jazz, or Rock 'n' Roll—chanties seem *capable* of representing ethnic White-ness, not least because the discourse has been saying that. Perhaps because individuals have used chanties to reaffirm ethnicity they have exaggerated or imitated these particular ethnic markers. The ethnic community that was initially drawn to reviving chanties—British folklorists, college glee singers, boating enthusiasts, Anglo folk revivalists and so forth—became the shaping force behind how future participants would perceive the tradition. It is only reasonable that a "White" singer would sing a chanty in a "White" way. This amounts to a degree of uniformity in outlook, interest, and approach, which gives chanty performance in the current era its particular ethnic and cultural cast. This situation adheres in spite of the smaller body of discourse in the Sea Music subculture and maritime museums, which goes on about the varied sort of men who sang chanties in the past and the genre's diverse roots. The chanty-singing within these circles, too, is unlikely to reflect the style and content of historical chanty-singing. The import of this is not that current chanty-singing practice is broken. The phenomenon of singing chanties for pleasure, in various interpretations, constitutes as valid a music-culture as any other. Rather, recognition of the perspectives that inform current chanty-sing-ing, its presentation, and its auxiliary discourse helps us to distinguish these from those we may find in texts from the nineteenth century.

Notes for Concluding Note

1 The parsing of "English" and "Irish" from American perspectives on whiteness is a messy issue that I do not wish to discuss. As such, a perception of chanties (or at least, much of the repertoire) as specifically Irish is another fascinating issue that must be neglected.
2 Personal communication, Oct. 2009

REFERENCES

Abbe, William A. Abbe. Diary aboard the ship *Atkins Adams*. Manuscript, New Bedford Whaling Museum (ODHS 485).

Abrahams, Roger D. Review of *Chanteying Aboard American Ships*, Frederick Pease Harlow. *Western Folklore* 22.3 (1963): 219–20.

———. *Deep The Water, Shallow the Shore*. 1974. Mystic, CT: Mystic Seaport Museum, 2002.

———. *Singing the Master: The Emergence of African American Culture in the Plantation South*. New York: Pantheon, 1992.

Adams, Nehemiah. *A Voyage Around the World*. Boston: Henry Hoyt, 1871.

Adams, Robert Chamblet. *On Board the Rocket*. Boston: D. Lothrop, 1879.

———. "Sailors' Songs." *New Dominion Monthly*, April 1876: 259–64.

Albee, Parker Bishop. *Letters from Sea, 1882–1901: Joanna and Lincoln Colcord's Seafaring Childhood*. Gardiner, ME: Tilbury House; Penobscot Marine Museum, 1999.

Alden, William Livingston. "Sailors' Songs." *Harper's New Monthly Magazine*, July 1882: 281–6.

Allen, Isaac. "Songs of the Sailor." *Oberlin Students' Monthly* 1.2 (December 1858): 46–9.

"Along the Color Line: Music and Art" *The Crisis* 8.6 (October 1914): 268–71.

American Sea Songs and Shanties. Edited by Duncan Emrich. Rounder, 2004. CD.

Anderson, Harold. "Menhaden Chanteys: An African American Maritime Legacy." *Maryland Marine Notes* 18.1 (Jan./Feb. 2000): 1–6.

Associated Harvard Clubs. *Book of Songs*. Chicago: Lakeside Press, 1916.

Beck, Horace. *Folklore and the Sea*. Mystic, CT: Mystic Seaport Museum, 1973.

Bennett, William Cox. *Songs for Sailors*. London: Henry S. King, 1872.

Bernard, D. H. "Sea Songs and Chanties." *The Nautical Magazine* 75.6 (June 1906). 431–5.

Bishop, Julia C. "'Dr Carpenter from the Harvard College in America': An Introduction to James Madison Carpenter and his Collection." *Folk Music Journal* 7.4 (1998): 402–20.

Bone, David William. *Capstan Bars*. Edinburgh: The Porpoise Press, 1931.

Bradford, John and Arthur Fagge. *Old Sea Chanties*. London: Metzler, 1904.

Broadwood, Lucy E. and A. H. Fox-Strangways. "Early Chanty-Singing and Ship-Music." *Journal of the Folk-Song Society* 8.32 (1928): 55–60.

Broadwood, Lucy E., Percy Grainger, Cecil J. Sharp, Ralph Vaughan Williams, Frank Kidson, J.A. Fuller-Maitland, and A.G. Gilchrist. "[Songs Collected by Percy Grainger]." *Journal of the Folk-Song Society* 3.12 (1908): 170–242.

Bullen, Frank T. *The Log of a Sea-Waif*. New York: D. Appleton, 1899.

Bullen, Frank T. and W. F. Arnold. *Songs of Sea Labour (Chanties)*. London: Swan, 1914.

Buryeson, Fred H. "Sea Shanties." *Coast Seamen's Journal*, June 23, 1909: 1–2, 10.

Campbell, Olive D. and Cecil J. Sharp. *English Folk Songs from the Southern Appalachians*. New York and London: G. P. Putnam's Sons, 1917.

"Canoeing." *Forest and Stream* 39.9 (September 1, 1892): 188.

Carpenter, James Madison. "Chanteys in the Age of Sail." *New York Times*, October 30, 1938: XX6.

_____. "Chanteys that 'Blow the Man Down.'" *New York Times*, July 26, 1931: 10, 15.

_____. "Forecastle Songs and Chanties." PhD diss., Harvard University, 1929.

_____. "Life Before the Mast: A Chantey Log." *New York Times*, July 19, 1931: SM8–9.

_____. "Lusty Chanteys from Long-dead Ships." *New York Times*, July 12, 1931: SM13, 23.

Carr, James Revell. *Hawaiian Music in Motion: Mariners, Missionaries, and Minstrels.* Urbana: University of Illinois, 2014.

_____. "Interpreted Authenticity: Chanteying in American Museums." Society for Ethnomusicology Annual Meeting, Detroit, MI, October 2001.

Carr Laughton, L. G. "Shantying and Shanties [part one]." *The Mariner's Mirror* 9.2 (February 1923): 48–55.

Carr Laughton, L. G. "Shantying and Shanties [part two]." *The Mariner's Mirror* 9.3 (March 1923): 66–74.

"Carrying the Sea Atmosphere Inland." *Shipping*, November 16, 1918: 13–5.

Clark, Arthur H. *The Clipper Ship Era.* New York and London: G.P. Putnam's Sons, 1910.

Clark, George Edward. *Seven Years of a Sailor's Life.* Boston: Adams, 1867.

Clayton, Paul and the Foc'sle Singers. *Foc'sle Songs and Shanties.* Folkways FA 2429, 1959. LP.

Cockrell, Dale. *Demons of Disorder: Early Blackface Minstrels and Their World.* Cambridge: Cambridge University Press, 1997.

Colcord, Joanna C. *Roll and Go: Songs of American Sailormen.* Indianapolis: Bobbs-Merrill, 1924.

_____. *Songs of American Sailormen.* New York: Norton, 1938.

Collins, James H. "Vikings of the Future." *St. Nicholas* 45.10 (August 1918): 881–4.

"Country and Colonial News." *The Musical Times*, May 1, 1913: 335–8.

Creighton, Helen. *Songs and Ballads from Nova Scotia.* 1932. New York: Dover, 1966.

Cruz, Jon. *Culture on the Margins: The Black Spiritual and the Rise of American Cultural Interpretation.* Princeton, NJ: Princeton University Press, 1999.

Dana, Richard Henry, Jr. *Two Years Before the Mast: A Personal Narrative of Life at Sea.* 1840. New York: Harper & Brothers, 1842.

Davis, Frederick J. and Ferris Tozer. *Sailors' Songs or "Chanties."* London: Boosey, n.d. [1887].

_____. *Sailors' Songs or "Chanties."* Second edition. London: Boosey, n.d. [1890].

_____. *Sailors' Songs or "Chanties."* Third edition. London: Boosey, n.d. [1891].

_____. *Sailors' Songs or "Chanties."* Revised edition. London: Boosey, n.d. [1927].

Doerflinger, William Main. *Shantymen and Shantyboys: Songs of the Sailor and Lumberman.* Macmillan: New York, 1951.

_____. *Songs of the Sailor and Lumberman.* Glenwood, IL: Meyerbooks, 1990.

Dow, George Francis. Letter from George Francis Dow of Marine Research Society, Salem, to F. P. Harlow, 21 June 1928. G. W. Blunt White Library, Mystic Seaport Museum.

"The Drunken Sailor." Narrated by Richard Hawley. BBC Radio 2, January 22, 2013.

Eckstorm, Fannie Hardy and Mary Winslow Smyth. *Minstrelsy of Maine: Folk-songs and Ballads of the Woods and the Coast.* Boston and New York: Houghton Mifflin, 1927.

Frank, Stuart M. Sea *Chanteys and Sailors' Songs: An Introduction for Singers and Performers, and a Guide for Teachers and Group Leaders*. Sharon, MA: The Kendall Whaling Museum, 2000.

Gilchrist, Annie G., Frank Kidson, Lucy E. Broadwood, Cecil J. Sharp, and J. A. Fuller-Maitland. "Sailors' Songs, Collected by Annie G. Gilchrist." *Journal of the Folk-Song Society* 2.9 (1906): 236–49.

Gordon, Robert Winslow. *Folk-songs of America*. New York: National Service Bureau, 1938.

_____. "Folk Songs of America: A Hunt on Hidden Trails." *New York Times*, January 2, 1927: SM3, 23.

_____. "Folk Songs of America: Work Chanteys." *New York Times*, January 16, 1927: SM7, 10.

Harker, David. *Fakesong: The Manufacture of British "Folksong" 1700 to the Present Day*. Milton Keynes: Oxford University Press, 1985.

Harlow, Frederick Pease. 1962. *Chanteying Aboard American Ships*. Mystic, CT: Mystic Seaport, 2004.

_____. "Chanteying Aboard American Ships." *The American Neptune* 8.2 (1948): 81–9.

_____. *The Making of a Sailor or Sea Life Aboard a Yankee Square-Rigger*. 1928. New York: Dover, 1988.

Haswell, George H. *Ten Shanties Sung on the Australian Run 1879*. Edited by Graham Seal. Mt. Hawthorn, W.A.: Antipodes Press, 1992.

Hatfield, James Taft. "Some Nineteenth Century Shanties." *Journal of American Folklore* 59.232 (1946): 108–13.

Hills, W. H., ed. *Students' Songs*. Thirteenth edition. Boston: Rand Avery, 1887.

Howard, Henry. "Manning the New Merchant Marine." *Pacific Marine Review* 15 (August 1918): 102–5.

Hubbard, W. L., ed. *History of American Music*. Toledo: Irving Squire, 1908.

Hugill, Stan. *The Bosun's Locker*. Todmorden, Yorkshire: David Herron, 2006.

Hugill, Stan. *Shanties and Sailors' Songs*. New York: Praeger, 1969.

_____. *Shanties from the Seven Seas: Shipboard Work-songs and Songs Used as Work-songs from the Great Days of Sail*. London: Routledge and Kegan Paul, 1961.

_____. *Shanties from the Seven Seas: Shipboard Work-songs and Songs Used as Work-songs from the Great Days of Sail*. Abridged edition. Mystic, CT: Mystic Seaport, 1994.

_____. *Songs of the Sea*. Maidenhead, U.K.: McGraw-Hill, 1977.

Hutchison, Percy Adams. "Sailors' Chanties." *Journal of American Folklore* 19.72 (Jan.–March 1906): 16–28.

Ipcar, Charles, ed. *Sea Songs of Cicely Fox Smith*. Richmond, ME: Charles Ipcar, 2010.

Jabbour, Alan and Julia C. Bishop. "The James Madison Carpenter Collection." *Folk Music Journal* 7.4 (1998): 399–401.

Jeffery, Walter. *A Century of Our Sea Story*. London: John Murray, 1900.

Jewell, J. Grey. *Among Our Sailors*. New York: Harper & Brothers, 1874.

Jones, Bessie and the Georgia Sea Island Singers. *Georgia Sea Island Songs*. New World Records, 1977. LP.

Keeler, Charles. *A Wanderer's Songs of the Sea*. San Francisco: A.M. Robertson, 1902.

Kellogg, Elijah. *The Ark of Elm Island*. Boston: Lee and Shepard, 1869.

_____. *A Strong Arm and a Mother's Blessing.* Boston: Lee and Shepard, 1880.

King, Stanton H. *King's Book of Chanties.* Boston: Oliver Ditson, 1918.

Kipling, Rudyard. "The Last Chanty." *The Pall Mall Magazine* 1.1 (1893): 129–32.

Kodish, Deborah G. "Introduction." In liner notes of *"Folk-songs of America": The Robert Winslow Gordon Collection, 1922–1932,* edited by Neil V. Rosenberg and Deborah G. Kodish, 3–14. Library of Congress, 1978. LP.

Lahee, Henry C. "Sailors' Chanteys." *The Sea Breeze* 13.1 (Oct. 1900): 13–4.

Lanier, Daniel and Vincent Reid. "Whalers' Shanties of Barouallie, St. Vincent: Observations on the Nature, Decline and Revival of a Unique Caribbean Maritime Tradition." *International Journal of Intangible Heritage* 2 (2007): 70–80.

Leslie, R. C. *A Sea Painter's Log.* London: Chapman & Hall, 1886.

Lloyd, Llewelyn C. "Folk-songs of the Sea: Shanties on the Gramophone." *Gramophone,* March 1927.

Lomax, Alan, rec. Albert Henry Rasmussen, London, April, 1955. England and Wales 1951–1958 Collection. Association for Cultural Equity. [http://www.culturalequity.org]

_____. *Bahamas 1935—Chanteys and Anthems from Andros and Cat Island.* Rounder, 1999. CD.

_____. Bright Light Quartet, Weems or Whitestone, Virginia, May, 1960. Southern U.S. 1959 and 1960 Collection. Association for Cultural Equity. [http://www.culturalequity.org]

_____. Captain Richard Maitland recordings of sea shanties, May, 1939. Washington, D.C.: Archive of Folk Culture, American Folklife Center, Library of Congress.

_____. Caribbean 1962 Collection. Association for Cultural Equity. [http://www.culturalequity.org]

_____. Georgia Sea Island Singers, St. Simons Island, Georgia, Oct, 1959. Southern U.S. 1959 and 1960 Collection. Association for Cultural Equity. [http://www.culturalequity.org]

Lomax, Alan, Zora Neale Hurston, and Mary Elizabeth Barnicle, rec. Recordings in the Bahamas. Alan Lomax, Zora Neale Hurston, and Mary Elizabeth Barnicle expedition collection. Washington, D.C.: Archive of Folk Culture, American Folklife Center, Library of Congress, 1935.

London, Jack. *The Son of the Wolf: Tales of the Far North.* New York: Grosset and Dunlap, 1900.

Lubbock, Basil. *Round the Horn Before the Mast.* London: John Murray, 1902.

Luce, Admiral Stephen Bleecker. *Naval Songs.* New York: Wm. A. Pond, 1883.

_____. *Naval Songs.* Second edition. New York: Wm. A. Pond, 1902.

MacKenzie, W. Roy. *Ballads and Sea Songs from Nova Scotia.* Cambridge: Harvard University Press, 1928.

Manchester Literary Club. *Papers of the Manchester Literary Club.* Vol. 21. Manchester: John Heywood, 1895.

Masefield, John, ed. *A Sailor's Garland.* London: Macmillan, 1906.

_____. "Sea-Songs." *Temple Bar,* January 1906: 56–80.

McQuade. James. *The Cruise of the Montauk to Bermuda, the West Indies, and Florida.* New York: Thomas R. Knox, 1885.

Mitchell, Wilmot Brookings, ed. *Elijah Kellogg: The Man and his Work*. Boston: Lee and Shepard, 1903.

Murray, James A. H., ed. *The Complaynt of Scotland*. 1549. London: N. Trübner, 1872.

NBC University of the Air. *Music of the New World: Handbook*. Vol. 3. New York: Southern Music Company. 1944.

"Official Chantey Singer." *New York Times*, January 27, 1918: 46.

"On Shanties." *Once a Week* 31 (August 1868): 92–3.

Palmer, Roy. *The Oxford Book of Sea Songs*. Oxford and New York: Oxford University Press, 1986.

Parrish, Lydia. *Slave Songs of the Georgia Sea Islands*. New York: Creative Age Press, 1942.

Patterson, J. E. "Sailors' Work Songs." *Good Words* 41.28 (June 1900): 391–7.

The Quid, or Tales of my Messmates. London: W. Strange, 1832.

Rasmussen, Albert Henry. *Sea Fever*. New York: Thomas Y. Crowell, 1952.

"Reviews and Notices of Books," *The Lancet*, May 5, 1906: 1253.

Robinson, John. "Half a Century at Sea." *The Bellman*, July 7, 1917: 10–4.

_____. "Songs of the Chanty-Man: I." *The Bellman*, July 14, 1917: 38–44.

_____. "Songs of the Chanty-Man: II." *The Bellman*, July 21, 1917: 66–72.

_____. "Songs of the Chanty-Man: III." *The Bellman*, July 28, 1917: 96–102.

_____. "Songs of the Chanty-Man: IV." *The Bellman*, Aug. 4, 1917: 123–8.

Runciman, James. *Skippers and Shellbacks*. London: Chatto and Windus, 1885.

Russell, W. Clark. "A Claim for American Literature" *The North American Review* 433 (February 1892): 138–50.

_____. "Jack's Courtship." *Longman's Magazine* 3 (November 1883): 1–43.

_____. *John Holdsworth: Chief Mate*. Vol. 1. London: Sampson Low, Marston, Low & Searle, 1875.

_____. "The Old Naval Song." *Longman's Magazine* 12 (June 1888): 180–91.

_____. *The Romance of Jenny Harlowe*. New York: D. Appleton, 1889.

_____. *Sailors' Language*. London: Sampson Low, Marston, Searle, & Rivington, 1883.

"Sailors' Shanties and Sea Songs." *Chambers's Journal* 4.311 (December 11, 1869): 794–6.

"Sailors' Songs." *The Riverside Magazine for Young People* 2.16 (April 1868): 185–7.

Sampson, John. *The Seven Seas Shanty Book*. London: Boosey, 1927.

Schreffler, Gibb. "Twentieth Century Editors and the Re-envisioning of Chanties: A Case Study of 'Lowlands'." *The Nautilus* 5 (2014): 7–51.

Scudder, Horace Elisha. *The Bodleys on Wheels*. Boston: Houghton, Osgood and Co., 1879.

"Sea Chanteys Kept Alive. Sailors' Club in London is Collecting and Preserving the Old Songs of Sail." *New York Times*, November 7, 1926: SM18.

"Shanty." In *A New English Dictionary on Historical Principles*, Vol. 8, part 2, edited by James A. H. Murray, Henry Bradley, and William A. Craigie, 626. Oxford: Clarendon Press, 1914.

Sharp, Cecil J. *English Folk-Chanteys*. London: Simpkin, Marshall, Hamilton, Kent & Co., 1914.

Sharp, Cecil J., A. G. Gilchrist, and Lucy E. Broadwood. "Sailors' Chanties." *Journal of the Folk-Song Society* 5.18 (1914): 31–44.

Sharp, Cecil J., A. G. Gilchrist, Lucy E. Broadwood, Frank Kidson, and Harry E. Piggott. "Sailors' Chanties." *Journal of the Folk-Song Society* 5.20 (1916): 297–315.

Shay, Frank. *American Sea Songs and Chanteys*. New York: Norton, 1948.

"Shipmate Will Brown." *The Riverside Magazine for Young People* 4.45 (September 1870): 402–4.

The Smart Set [New York], November 1905.

Smith, Cicely Fox. *A Book of Shanties*. London: Methuen, 1927.

Smith, Laura Alexandrine. *The Music of the Waters*. London: Kegan, Paul, Trench & Co., 1888.

"Songs of the Sea." *Atlantic Monthly* 2.9 (July 1858): 152–6.

"Suburban Concerts," *The Musical Times*, April 1, 1906: 262.

Terry, Richard Runciman. "Sailor Shanties (I)." *Music and Letters* 1.1 (1920): 35–44.

_____. "Sailor Shanties (II)." *Music and Letters* 1.3 (1920): 256–68.

_____. "Sea Songs and Shanties." *Proceedings of the Royal Music Association* 11.41 (1915): 135–40.

_____. *The Shanty Book: Part I*. London: J. Curwen & Sons, 1921.

_____. *The Shanty Book: Part II*. London: J. Curwen & Sons, 1926.

_____. *The Way of the Ship: Sailors, Shanties and Shantymen*. Tucson, AZ: Fireship Press, 2009.

United States Merchant Marine Commission. *Report of the Merchant Marine Commission, Together with the Testimony Taken at the Hearings*. Vol. 1. Washington: Government Printing Office, 1905.

Walser, Robert Young. "'Here We Come Home in a Leaky Ship!': The Shanty Collection of James Madison Carpenter." *Folk Music Journal* 7.4 (1998): 471–95.

_____. "The Shantyman's Canon." MA thesis, Univ. of Wisconsin, Madison, 1995.

Walton, Ivan H. with Joe Grimm. *Windjammers: Songs of the Great Lakes Sailors*. Detroit: Wayne State University, 2002.

Whall, William Boultbee. "Real Sea Songs." *The Nautical Magazine* 80.6 (Dec. 1908): 546–9.

_____. "Sea Melody—I." *The Nautical Magazine* [Glasgow] 76.1 (July 1906): 28–36.

_____. "The Sea Shanty." *Yachting Monthly*, October 1906: 448–52.

_____. *Sea Songs and Shanties*. Fourth edition. Glasgow: J. Brown and Son, 1920.

_____. *Ships, Sea Songs and Shanties*. Glasgow: Brown, Son and Ferguson, 1910.

_____. *Ships, Sea Songs and Shanties*. Second edition, enlarged. Glasgow: J. Brown & Son, 1912.

_____. *Ships, Sea Songs and Shanties*. Third edition, enlarged. Glasgow: J. Brown & Son, 1913.

Wheeler, Mary. *Steamboatin' Days: Folk Songs of the River Packet Era*. Baton Rouge: Louisiana State University Press, 1944.

Whitmarsh, H. Phelps. "The Chantey-man." *Harper's Monthly Magazine*, Jan. 1903: 319–23.

Williams, James H. "The Sailors' 'Chanties'." *The Independent* [New York], July 8, 1909: 76–83.

Winick, Stephen D. "'Sung with Gusto by the Men': A Unique Recording of 'The Leaving of Liverpool' in the AFC Archive." *Folklife Center News* 30.3/4 (2008): 3–12.

www.ingramcontent.com/pod-product-compliance
Lightning Source LLC
Chambersburg PA
CBHW061149040426
42445CB00013B/1628